Visual Cultures and Critical Theory

For Noah and Morgan – our lovely little angels

Visual Cultures and Critical Theory

Patrick Fuery and Kelli Fuery

First published in Great Britain in 2003 by
Arnold, a member of the Hodder Headline Group,
338 Euston Road, London NW1 3BH

http://www.arnoldpublishers.com

Distributed in the United States of America by
Oxford University Press Inc.
198 Madison Avenue, New York, NY10016

British Library Cataloguing-in-Publication Data
A catalogue record for this title is available from the British Library

British Library Cataloguing in Publication Data
A catalog record for this title is available from the Library of Congress

ISBN 0 340 80747 4 (hb)
ISBN 0 340 80748 2 (pb)

2 3 4 5 6 7 8 9 10

Typeset by Phoenix Photosetting, Chatham, Kent
Printed and bound in India.

What do you think about this book? Or any other Arnold title?
Please send your comments to feedback.arnold@hodder.co.uk

Contents

Acknowledgements

Many people are involved with the writing of any book and this is very much the case here. Our publishers were supportive and positive about the idea of this book, which was encouraging in all the appropriate stages of writing. In particular, we would like to thank Lesley Riddle for her initial help and friendly manner in dealing with all our queries and requests. Her suggestions at the commencement of this project were insightful and welcome. Our thanks go to Alexia Chan, who provided a smooth transition towards the end of the project. She offered understanding just where publishers need to without any compromise to the progress of the work. Thanks also to Colin Goodlad for his warmth, support and good humour.

In terms of academic stimulus and general banter, there are several whom we would like to thank. To our colleagues at Royal Holloway, University of London and at Curtin University, for their support. For the love of film, art, television and generally looking we thank Sam Tarlington, who happily spent many a night on Oxford Street just watching; Robyn Wagner who possesses a similar tenacity and enthusiasm for the saga of the screen as her sister; Margaret Mills who, through her friendship and care, has always given much in all of our discussions and of herself. Also to our families – their love, encouragement and interest in this book helped it move along.

And finally, for our little Noah – who without knowing it provided an unshakeable deadline and a much-anticipated sight on which to set our eyes.

A Note on Images

A book on visual cultures inevitably needs to refer to a great many images. However, we felt that any attempt to include all the images would be unwieldy and, perhaps even more disadvantageous, might restrict the concepts and issues to very specific examples. Therefore where possible we have included a reference to a web page where the images can be found. These will often direct the reader to other examples, which is very much in keeping with the spirit of the book. We have also included a list of some useful gallery pages and film reference sites. These will provide more examples and sources of reference.

Hyperlinks

Galleries referred to throughout the book:

http://www.nationalgallery.org.uk/collection/default.htm

http://www.tate.org.uk/modern/default.htm

http://www.artchive.com/ftp_site.htm

http://www.mcu.es/prado/index_eng.html

http://www.louvre.fr/louvrea.htm

http://www.rijksmuseum.nl/

http://www.uffizi.firenze.it/welcomeE.html

http://www.reemst.com/calvin_and_hobbes/

For all films referred to in all chapters:

http://www.imdb.com/

INTRODUCTION

There is a scene in one of the early episodes of the television series *The Sopranos* where Tony Soprano, one of the most powerful men in the Mafia, sits in the waiting room before his analysis session with his psychiatrist. He looks around the room, a curious figure (a mixture of masculine power and nervousness), before his eyes, and then our own gaze (through the camera), settles on a painting hung on the wall. It looks innocuous enough; a generic and relatively bland picture of a barn and some trees, but Tony's gaze insists on looking at it. We, the spectator, are made to look at it with this same degree of intensity. We peer into the image because the intensity of Tony's gaze tells us there is something significant here. A few moments later, in the session, Tony becomes agitated and asks Dr Melfi, his analyst, why she has the picture on the wall. She responds saying that it is only a picture and asks why it bothers him so much. At this all of the force of Tony Soprano explodes and he rants that it is a far from innocent picture, and insists that it is a trap – a psychoanalytic trap. He tells Dr Melfi that she shouldn't have such traps on the wall, and speaks of how much it affects his mind to see such an image.

In this scene, and it is beautifully done, we witness one of the fundamental issues of the image and the formation of what has come to be termed 'visual culture'. The image of the barn and trees is just that, and it may well have been hung on the wall simply to take blankness from the space, or add some cheer to a stressful environment. It is the sort of image that we all encounter, perhaps do not even register, every day – from doctors' waiting rooms to bus stops, from the calendars we hang in the kitchen, to the countless postcards of seasides or famous buildings, to the hundreds of pictures we flick past in a magazine. And most of the time these images will slip from our eyes, no more noticed than a colour of a fence, a curtain, or a stranger's face in the street. But now and then the image seems to be more powerful, more demanding and relevant, and we are drawn to it. Part of the complexity is figuring out why some images do this more than others, why an image can do this at one moment and not another, and how we might share such an experience with others. From the almost unseen to the insistent, these images are the constitutive elements of a visual culture; how we become spectators of them is what locates us within a visual culture. Between these three elements – image, culture, spectator – exists a powerful and complex matrix of processes and relationships.

Before we go any further, let us take up a second image. In a different way this image illustrates a similar point that is operating in Tony Soprano's compulsion to the painting on the wall. In the sixteenth century, Europe was devastated by a series of plagues, which were seen as apocalyptic omens. Cities and countries lost millions of lives, and the sensibility of the cultures was shaped by the ever-present sense of death. In 1516 Grünewald's *The Isenheim Altarpiece*[a1] appears. Like so many paintings of its type it shows the body of the dead Christ, the mourning followers surrounding. What is striking about this body, however, is that it bears the sores and blisters of the plague. Grünewald has taken a current event, something that has consumed the population of Europe, and shaped the consciousness of the culture, and transposed it onto the figure of Christ. It is essential to Christian belief that Christ died on the cross, and yet here is an image that shows him with the plague. It is an interesting image because it dramatically demonstrates that no matter how powerful the image, it can be shaped and altered to fit within a particular cultural order. Furthermore, as we shall see throughout this book, it is not simply the creator of the image doing this, but the spectator necessarily shifts and contorts the image.

This is one of the fundamental issues of visual cultural studies – the inter-relationship between the image and cultural moments and processes. Just as Tony Soprano shapes the image to fit within his own cultural context (the violent world of the Mafia and its paranoid consequences, the death of friends,[2] the feelings of entrapment, and so on), so Grünewald has shaped an image to be more relevant to his contemporary audience. From a clichéd and mass-produced painting to the body of Christ, there is a constant force of relations between image and culture. When we speak of visual cultures here this is part of what we mean; it is the complex interaction between a cultural order of things (including the sense-making processes), the generating, sustaining and rendering visible of images, and the creation of the spectator. It is important to recognize that images do not simply exist – they must be made visible. This rendering visible of the image is part of the creation of a spectator. It is how images come to exist, and, significantly, how they come to be seen as meaningful and the bearers of meanings.

We must be careful not to simply see this as a one-directional relationship – of images being used to respond to certain cultural issues and concerns. For there is also another relationship, flowing, as it were, in the opposite direction. This is the way in which the images actually shape cultural processes. It is perhaps an impossibility to map out such relationships, because inevitably they are built up over time, sifted through by different cultural groups and individuals, made relevant and irrelevant across moments in history. What is of greater interest here is to note that such things do in fact take place; and in doing so participate in the formation of visual cultures. To give an idea of such a process, however, consider the formations of the beautiful body, or the images of seduction. These sorts of images change in a remarkably short space of time or rapidly across cultures. A fundamental part of this process is the ways in which images themselves come to define the beautiful, the abject and the seductive.

This idea, that the relationship of the image and culture is far more than merely a system of representing orders and ideologies, and more embedded in a vast and complex set of agendas and relationships, informs the use of the term 'visual culture' here. In other words, we see visual culture as denoting the complexities of image and culture, including this drive to render the image as significant, and the culturally significant as an image. A key component in this is the spectator. Because we see visual culture as a dynamic and ever-changing set of relations, it is important to note that the spectator is equally dynamic and constantly shifting. The spectator is an agency of the image as well as the culture; he/she cannot be passive, but must always be located within a range of forces that determine, and are determined by, the image. So these three elements of spectator, image and culture, shape each other in a system of reciprocity.

This book takes up these issues within a particular context. Over the last hundred years or so there has been a rich and complex series of ideas that have come to question many of the ideas and systems of thought in the Western world. It is termed critical theory here, but it is a heterogeneous group, and sometimes the key figures are more antagonistic to one another than unified. It is important to note this, for it would be erroneous to see the theorists discussed here as a united front. What they do have in common, however, is this large-scale questioning of the order of things. From history to language, from culture to the unconscious, from gender and sexuality to philosophies about being; these thinkers engaged in a radical and detailed examination of the ways in which thought and culture have operated, and how they have continued to operate.

We have concentrated on some of the key theorists, but have had to leave out some others; and unfortunately this does have the consequence of seeming to canonize some. However, this is not an attempt to privilege some over others, and certainly not an aim to continue to create a canon of critical thinkers. Our selection of theorists has been made on a number of choices, and at the same time we acknowledge that omissions create worrying holes. What these theorists do is provide us with some indication of the range and scope of ideas that have been developed. With this in mind the reader is encouraged to go wider and engage in others that we have had to leave out because of the limitations of space.

It is significant that none of the theorists is directly concerned with the visual (none, that is to say, would call her/himself someone 'trained' in the visual arts). And yet all of them, in their works and ideas, have had a major impact on the development of the new discipline of visual cultural studies. This has been a two-way relationship. The theories and ideas developed have profoundly altered the analysis of the image. At the same time we can notice a strikingly large amount of visual reference and theorizing within these works. So even if these theorists did not set out to develop a theory of the image, their ideas have been instrumental in shaping contemporary debates on the image. And, perhaps even more significantly, the visual has proven to be an essential part of their theorizing. We also selected the theorists because they have been so influential in many areas of the humanities – they have managed to bring to question the very foundation of humanities as an activity. A significant part of their impact has been to reconfigure the humanities, its subject matter and systems of analysis. This has had the consequence of positioning the image as a key factor in a great many disciplines.

These, then, are two of the organizational principles for this book: the investigation of some of the key relationships between image, culture and the spectator, and the links between some of the major critical theories and the visual (including how the visual has been employed by them). There is a third underlying theme in this book, which we have employed to keep things as manageable as possible. This is the use of certain key themes to focus the material. These have been chosen for a number of reasons. First, they are often indicative of the ideas and issues that the theories themselves have engaged in; second, they are representative of some of the complexities of the ideas (including the challenge to the disciplines themselves); third, they offer the opportunity to reinterpret the ideas from a new perspective. These themes include power, subjectivity, desire, textuality, abjection and, of course, culture.

The book, then, can be approached from a number of different angles. It can be used to work through some of the major theories in the humanities in recent times, employing visual examples to understand the ideas; it can be used to explore some of the issues of the emerging field of visual cultural studies; it can be used to explore how the concepts from critical theory can be developed for the analysis of the image; and it can be used to see some of the key themes of critical theory and cultural studies. We have tried to work through these aspects by using as wide a range of visual media as possible. Inevitably, however, some have been more 'privileged' than others. One of the strategies we have adopted is to make reference to certain visual media (such as public spaces and architecture) and encourage the reader to develop the examples further. Once more this is more to do with the limitations of size than actual significance of the subject matter. We have made the texts purposefully broad, and have extended, when possible, the idea of the visual text. For example, we make reference to the body, and parts of the body, to the frame and borders, to spaces and edges. This is because, in keeping with the spirit of the critical theories, we believe it is important to see the visual as exceeding the image itself.

We live in a world of the image. The very idea of the self, the ways in which we make sense of the world, the means by which we communicate, have all become invested in, and developed through, the visual. In many ways images have replaced the word as the defining aspect of cultural identity, and at the same time they have become part of the attempt to create a global culture. The rapidly developing discipline of visual cultural studies has become the key area for examining the issues of the image. The role of this book is to consider the intersection between visual cultures and the most significant developments in critical theory over the last fifty years. This includes issues and concepts from psychoanalysis, philosophy, cultural theory, postmodernism, feminism, queer theory, gender studies and narrative theory. *Visual Cultures and Critical Theory* aims to provide an interplay between the image and recent developments in the humanities. To see how these organizing ideas are developed in the book, the following is a short summary of each of the chapters.

The first chapter, 'Investing in power and the body', takes up a number of the fundamental concerns in the works of Michel Foucault. We open with this chapter because Foucault offers such an extraordinary analytic depth to the understanding of how cultural processes operate. In doing so he provides us with the opportunity to explore one of the major themes of the book – how we become positioned as spectators and the sorts of relationships that are developed in this. To understand this we discuss Foucault's ideas on power and formations of knowledge. These are complex and intricate ideas, and Foucault spends a lifetime of work exploring the nature of them. What he develops is no less than a radical perspective on the subject devised through and in power. We take up these ideas and consider them in terms of the subject as spectator – that is, the positions of power relations that take place when we look at an image. In this Foucauldian sense what takes place whenever we look at an image is that we are located in a certain way by that image.

The first half of this chapter, then, takes up Foucault's ideas on what he terms power/knowledge. We consider the cultural forces at hand in order to form the image and how these forces also operate to create a certain type of (compliant) spectator. Foucault was always more than a recorder and detailer of such power relations in the social order, and attempted to offer a perspective of resistance as well. In this spirit we outline how the spectator can be made compliant by the image, and yet also the ways in which he/she resists such positioning. This struggle between spectator and image is the fundamental aspect of a Foucauldian reading of visual culture. The second half of the chapter explores this in greater detail, taking up the idea of different types of bodies. We do this in part because it is such a representative theme of Foucault (he wrote extensively about the body) and in part because it is an essential part of the discipline of visual cultural studies.

The second chapter, 'Seeing the self in the Baroque mirror', deals with the psychoanalytic ideas of Jacques Lacan and some of their Freudian foundations. Lacan was profoundly influenced by the visual and even when he did not make direct reference to it there is often the sense of the image at hand. This is somewhat surprising given that so much of Lacanian theory is concerned with speech and language. To this end we have tried to redress the balance, and to show just how significant the visual is to Lacan's ideas and style. We take up a particular inflection of the visual to explore this idea that Lacan not only refers to the visual, but also has a style of writing (and speech) that was strongly influenced by the Baroque.

We take up some of the key ideas in Lacanian theory, in particular the formation of subjectivity, the operation of the unconscious, and processes of desire. These are set against a number of different sets of images, including painting, the body, cinema and the mirror. One of the key ideas is how Lacan explores the reflexivity of the self, and in doing so locates the theme of the mirror as an integral part of the formation of the subject. More than this, however, we wish to argue that the visual is an ongoing part of the questioning, assertion, collapse and strengthening of subjectivity. This is what makes Lacan one of the most important theorists in recent times. For he offers the possibility of understanding what it is to have subjectivity, and how such a status is constantly problematized. The style of the Baroque is discussed in part because it seems to be such a significant and yet neglected part of Lacan's work. Here is a style of art – indeed a style of thinking – with which Lacan aligns himself and yet is so rarely referred to. There is something to be said in the argument that if we understand the Baroque then the style of Lacan becomes a little easier to grasp. The chapter closes with a discussion of celebrity, for in this cultural phenomenon we observe a conflation of these themes of desire, the subject and the primacy of the image.

The third chapter, 'Transgression, abjection and the body', deals with the psychoanalyst and philosopher Julia Kristeva. We take up a particular line of thought from Kristeva, that of the body and how it functions in terms of the image. We are particularly concerned with the ideas involving the cultural order and the processes of disruption. These disruptive moments, examined through the body and the visual, are seen as both transgressive and creative; they are the spaces in the cultural order that actually allow change and revolution to take place.

This chapter looks especially at how Kristeva deals with the abject (which is both the unnameable horror and something that is deeply fascinating) and the various systems of disruption. We are particularly interested in the ways in which images, through visual cultures, do more than act as representations of the body and its various guises (including the abject). We also consider the very capacity of the image to disrupt and disturb the cultural order, as well as the ways in which it is managed and controlled.

The fourth chapter, 'From parasitology to spectres', takes up the ideas of the philosopher Jacques Derrida and his notion of deconstruction. Derrida, like all of the theorists here, is a complex thinker and there are always the difficulties of making what is a highly specialized discipline – in this case philosophy – accessible to the more generalist reader. What is particularly relevant in Derrida's case is that much of what he is dealing with has broad implications across a range of disciplines. Often when Derrida is at his most specific, digging away at what might appear to be an obscure philosophical text, is when he is in fact offering insights into a much larger issue. This is also the case with the whole sense of deconstruction itself. Part of the concern in this chapter is to see how various aspects of deconstruction can be applied to the analysis of the image. And, as with all the chapters, how significant the image has been in the theoretical developments.

The chapter on Derrida commences with some of the ways in which Derrida has spoken of deconstruction, particularly in terms of a parasite and virus. We consider how this positioning of an analytic technique as something internal to the discourse under analysis can be compared to the image in various cultural contexts. Our example is the ways in which terrorism and the state vie for the power of the image in the cultural order of things. We then consider some of Derrida's key motifs that have strong visual connotations, including the frame and the double. The chapter concludes by considering two images that seem highly appropriate to the whole deconstructionalist method – that is, the spectre and the mirror. Through these we examine the idea of unconfirmed status (of ideas, things and subjects) and the forces of reflexivity. In many ways these sum up so much of what Derrida deals with throughout his works.

The fifth chapter, 'Spectator, culture, image', takes up the ideas of the semiotician Roland Barthes. Perhaps more than any of the other thinkers considered in this book,

Barthes stays closest to the text. He is interesting in part because he is someone who moves from a strongly linguistic and literary position in his early works to a more visually driven one in the latter. (This is of course almost too general to be fair to Barthes, but his early works are notable for their literary interests, such as the reading of Balzac in *S/Z*, to his final book on photography.) Barthes also shows us a thinker moving from a structuralist position (heavily influenced by the linguistic theories of Saussure and the anthropologist Lévi-Strauss) to a post-structuralist one (with evidence of Lacan, Kristeva and even Derrida).

Our concern in this chapter is to work through the two aspects that have been crucial to the development of semiotics. The first of these is to locate the cultural contexts of the sign and signification. Simply put, this is the idea that meaning can only ever operate within a social structure, and that all significations emerge from, and return to, culture. The second crucial development in these terms is the idea of the reader/spectator as a creative part of the text. This includes Barthes' ideas on pleasure and *jouissance* (that moment of excess and orgasm that threatens the social order), of the death of the author and, finally, the sites of resistance in reading against the cultural order. We also take the idea of cultural narratives (that is, the ways in which a culture is narrativized) as a form of visualizing, which includes the creation of images to form and sustain cultural representation.

The final chapter, 'Invisibility and hallucination: the state of the image in the postmodern world', takes up a number of different theorists in order to offer a certain perspective on what has happened to the image in the postmodern world. It is not so much a summarizing of the image and postmodernism (another project lies there), but some observations on how the image has been problematized. To this end we look to the otherness of the image – its invisibilities, surfaces and hallucinations. This final chapter looks at the significance of absence to the image, suggesting that perhaps this is one of the directions that critical theory leads us – that is, to the beyond of the image. We are also concerned with this idea of the image as it operates in various cultural contexts. The emphasis is on the authenticity of images, and the political powers that come into play between culture and spectator. This recurring theme of the book is illuminated in quite a different fashion here.

The first part of this chapter takes up some of the ideas from the philosophical and psychoanalytic approaches of Gilles Deleuze and Félix Guattari. We focus on their idea of the rhizome, with its emphasis on surface and network, in order to understand the image and visual cultures from a different perspective. The image as rhizome leads to a contesting of not only what an image is, but also how power and subjectivity are necessary components (of both activity and analysis) of the image itself. The second part of the chapter takes up a similar theme, this time in terms of the philosopher and cultural analyst Jean Baudrillard. We concentrate on his ideas of simulation and simulacra. (Space limits our discussion of Baudrillard, and somewhat unfortunately we could not include Baudrillard's own works on the visual. We chose to focus on the wider theories of

Baudrillard – that is, ones that inform a great deal of his work – in order to keep with the spirit of the book.) The final section of this chapter takes up ideas on invisibility and hallucination, gender and race, to show how the image is manipulated in different cultural contexts. This is done in order to demonstrate the effectiveness of the different theories in uncovering such visual distortions.

Notes

1 Where possible we have included hyperlinks to images referred to throughout the book. A complete list of these images appears at the end of each chapter. These are designated by letters.

2 In this particular episode the head of the 'family' is dying of cancer; Tony reads the tree in the image as eaten away from the inside out.

a Grünewald, *The Isenheim Altarpiece*
http://kfki.nu/~arthp/html/g/grunewald/zisenhei/1view

Chapter One

INVESTING IN POWER AND THE BODY

Foucault and the visual

INVESTING POWER IN THE IMAGE

Why power? And why power and the image? When we look at images are we interacting with relations of power? Have we entered into an economy of power that positions us and how we view what we look at? Aren't we just looking? We look at ourselves every day, in the mirror, and for the most part we are consciously aware of nothing except a projected reflection. When we go to an art gallery or read a magazine, look at photos or even when we watch images on film or television, we are engaging with other images and forming investments of power. The two constants in each of the above situations are you, as spectator, and the image. It is this change from you-as-human-being to you-as-spectator that involves issues and relations of power within any interaction with the image.

For Michel Foucault, power was a means to an end. Foucault was not primarily interested in analysing or critiquing power, as for him power (as a freestanding socio-cultural force) did not exist prior to an interactive relationship. Rather, for Foucault, it was the subject, more specifically the construction of human beings into subjects, that was his main research objective. Power was only 'activated' once a power relationship had been constructed and engaged with. Foucault viewed power as a technique or mechanism to be used in working out why and how we become subjects. 'My objective, instead, has been to create a history of the different modes by which, in our culture, human beings are made subjects. My work has dealt with three modes of objectification which transform human beings into subjects' (Foucault 1983a: 208). By arguing that a subject invests power in an image, we look more towards the objectivizing of the subject from the perspective of the image and the resistance a spectating[1] subject produces in meeting and refusing such objectification. What is of interest here is how these power relations are produced and why they are produced to create certain subjectivity with specific reference to any image.

In order to use power as a tool to analyse the subject and how we become subjects, Foucault suggested a new economy of power relations. 'It consists of taking the forms of resistance against different forms of power as a starting point … Rather than analyzing power from the point of view of its internal rationality, it consists of analyzing power relations through the antagonism of strategies' (Foucault 1983a: 211). We can adopt this approach in finding out what power relations are involved in visual cultures, by looking at various oppositions such as resistances to power relations, or any attempts that are made to separate aspects that comprise power relations. This tells us more about power relationships, their function and effect, instead of merely outlining certain circumstances and situations wherein power operates. Identifying only what power relations are and what types exist highlights little about the subjects involved and any subjectivity produced by them. Additionally, this method of analysis emphasizes the most fundamental aspect of all power relations, that being how power is practised within a relationship. Directing this towards the image, we aim to sketch out what aspects are involved in forming types of power relations and essentially the significance this has for the spectating subject within visual cultures. Looking for the interrelationship and interaction that exists between subject and the image, aids the examination of how power relations between the two are constructed, played out and contested.

Questioning the status of the individual: struggles of power

Foucault's examination of power is complex and involved, as what ultimately drives his analysis is the new definition of an already socially current concept. Foucault takes the concept of power, redefines it and reshapes it so that he ends up with a different agenda contained within the same term. One of the ways in which he achieves this is through discussing what his version of power is not, and he does this through attacking what he terms 'power struggles'. These power struggles oppose and resist Foucault's typology of power, and on this basis they are criticizing power as a tool – what Foucault calls a 'form of power', not particular establishments or social classes – although this is not to deny that forms of power exist in these domains. Present commonalities between these struggles all circle around the issue and status of the subject, such as the notion of the subject as individual, the concept of individualization and the effects of power specific to subjection.

Foucault summarily identifies aspects of struggles as those 'which question the status of the individual ... struggles against the "government of individualization" ... struggles against the privileges of knowledge ... struggles revolve around the question: Who are we?' (Foucault 1983a: 212). Struggles then deal with the various effects of the exercise of power and for the most part are primarily concerned with attacking any form of power that attempts to govern the individual and prevent him or her from becoming a subject. However, viewing these power struggles from a different perspective suggests that the subject resists not only a prescription of individuality from the state but also resists the seduction of such conformity and homogeneity that the totalization of the subject yields. In terms of visual cultures, the spectating subject struggles against the seduction of the image – the seduction of being placed, of being told how and what to view. The current popularity of 'real life' television programmes attests to a viewer demographic succumbing to such a seduction of the image. From *Survivor* to *Temptation Island* to *Big Brother*, each television programme prescribes viewing places for the home viewer through constructing a strict narrative out of the power relations that develop between the game show participants. These programmes are not designed for the critical subject, instead they rely on the seduction within the image – being told what is meaningful is easier that assessing it critically for oneself. Thus power struggles comprise two sides, both centred on the creation of a particular subjectivity.

Foucault identifies three types of struggle – against domination, exploitation and subjection. While Foucault does not relate these forms of power struggle specifically to the image, they are concerned with the discourse of the subject and the creation of subjectivity. We can involve this discourse and its structure to examine how the subject views and interacts with the image, specifically with respect to issues of management and governmentality.

DOMINANCE

The subject has to struggle with the dominance of the image. The image dominates through the privilege of the institution-as-state. 'State' here meaning the prevailing conditions and mitigating factors that aim to individualize a subject. For our purposes, the state can function as those physical places where images are viewed or engaged with and the conceptual frame in which any image is viewed. The art gallery states 'this is art', the cinema states 'this is film'; the dominance of these images stemming from the autocratic and managerial discourses the institution-as-state establishes and practises. This form of totalitarian discourse is purported by the social order and is strengthened through a continuation of lack of rebellion and resistance from society. Within each visual medium there are images that contest the medium itself. Not only is the subject struggling against the dominance of the image but the images are struggling against other images. For example, David Lynch's *Mulholland Drive* (2002) defies conventional linear narrative and character development to produce a film that, in form, differs radically from other films. Yet much of the film's content and plot lines are markedly similar to other Lynch films. Thematically, *Blue Velvet* (1986), *Lost Highway* (1997) and *Wild at Heart* (1990) are other Lynch films that deal with chaos in morality and atypical representations of love and American society. Given that *Mulholland Drive* was originally intended as a pilot for a new television series, there are many similarities with *Twin Peaks*, Lynch's previous television series. In particular the character of Naomi Watts is templated on Sheryl Lee's character, Laura Palmer. In *Twin Peaks* Lynch uses Sheryl Lee to play both Laura Palmer and her cousin Madeline, as he does in *Mulholland Drive* where Naomi Watts plays two characters – Betty Elms and Diane Selwyn. This undermines the concept of double identity through exploiting issues of representation. Investing power in this type of image, as well as the montage, is to recognize its difference and liminal positioning compared with other films. Ironically, to invest in a film like Lynch's is to be seduced into his world of disorder and unrest while at the same time allowing one's subjectivity to be governed by it.

Films such as *Sorority Brothers* (Wolodarksy 2002), the *Scary Movie* series (Wayans 2000; Wayans 2001; Zucker 2003) and *Not Another Teen Movie* (Zucker 2001) dominate through their social discursive position as firm representations of attitudes present in phallocentric Western culture. These films seek no criticality from their audiences, there are no spaces invested by themselves for creative interpretation; instead these films seek a compliant investment of power from the individual. In terms of the image as state, these films seek the reflection and support in the maintenance of dominant ideology from its governed individuals. The governed subject who enjoys these films enjoys resting in the folds of dominant culture and is seduced by images that enforce it.

Seduction by the image is not always a negative process and is not limited to banal representations of right-wing culture. Using painting as an example, specifically here in the Renaissance period, lovers of Crivelli, Botticelli, Mantegna and Tura[a] form an investment of power in these images that reflects a subjectivity that locates them in proximity to these images. This form of investment is also made in response to the seduction of the image, but to a different effect. The image remains meaningful through recognition and subscription to its discourse, as with the teenage films. The more the image is interpreted as being important and powerful in its given visual field, the more seductive it becomes and the less it is met with spectator resistance. In this way an investment of power serves to strengthen the seduction of the image and ultimately its totalizing form. This is not to suggest that individuals of society are ineffectual and weak-minded, but rather to highlight and expose the fact that those investments of power in an image are heterogeneous. Being fond of a particular type of image doesn't necessarily negate other typologies of images being attractive, or that images found attractive bind you steadfast to a solitary subjectivity. What it indicates is that an investment of power along these seductive lines produces a reflective mode of subjectivity that responds to the dominance of the image with minimal resistance. In this way, the power struggle with dominance is a fundamental component to the formation of visual cultures.

Read differently, a strong, Western, culturally ubiquitous image like the crucifixion of Christ demands a higher level of resistance.[b] The image of Christ in church compared to the image of Christ on a children's Easter cartoon or in the renaissance section of the National Gallery, London, asks for a different type of investment of power from the subject. In church, commitment to (and engagement with) the image of Christ is fundamental to the faith and livelihood of the religious individual. Here the individual seeks a conscious domination formed through inviting Christ into his or her life specifically to control and guide it. The crucifixion functions as a synecdoche for a particular religious denomination and as such, an individual refusing to subscribe to the prescribed viewing position that such an image suggests is to greater define their subjectivity as critical spectator.

Power relations are effected and maintained through their invisible practice and deficient self-reflexive apparatus in socio-cultural 'state' places like cinemas, art galleries and personal living rooms. Power relations operate as expressions of powerful truths that are part of the construction of the discourse of the image. This form of domination present in visual cultures is social. In this power struggle of dominance, the subject resists and opposes a homogeneous social positioning that seeks to unify all individuals into a governed position. To meet all resistances and struggles of forms of power, the spectating subject, as a critical thinker, produces a mirror or a considered form of investment in the image. They imagine the image on their own terms and oppose its seduction. The image – whether it is painting, film or television – is seen not for what it is, but what it is for the subject. The spectating subject, as opposed to a seduced subject, does not want to be dominated by the image; but if the individual is seduced by the dominance of the image, their investment of power takes the form of reflection. The spectating subject does not want to be exploited by the image through any form of social dominance that the image constructs. If the individual is seduced by the social positioning of the image, they choose to reflect it by investing a typology of power that affirms and seeks to solidify the image's place and relation to the state (whether the state be cinema, art or popular culture). The power struggle of dominance is hard to work through precisely because it requires a lack of questioning from the subject in order to operate successfully. In order for power to dominate, the subject needs to be dominated via seduction but this does not always occur. As a spectating subject, investment into any mode of communication or signification, especially visual cultures, is based on a critical approach to power.

The spectating subject is not seduced by the image and adopts a critical perspective regarding the image, as well as their interaction with it, their investment of power forming a different form of reflection. The individual as a spectating subject is, in response to the image and its 'state', reflecting liberation from the type of individualization that the image as government prescribes. The image is appropriated and reviewed via the desire of the subject. The spectating subject's discovery within this investment is not the answer to 'What are we?' but a refusal of the management and governing that constructs a viewing status when the image asks 'What are we?' Part of the function of the visual in cultures is to allow a struggle with forms of power, and thus becomes an investment of power born from struggle.

EXPLOITATION

[F]orms of exploitation that separate individuals from what they produce

(Foucault 1983a: 212)

Domination of the subject is a social struggle; the image dominates and seduces that individual via the state strategies of management and government. The struggle that the spectating subject is faced with is the consequence of their investment of power. To be dominated is to be seduced and remain as a governed individual in relation to the image. To become a critical and spectating subject in a power relation with an image, or visual cultures in general, is to refuse the constructed viewing position and remain at a distance. This distance is part of separating the individual from what they produce.

In separating each struggle we hope to found a cogent understanding of what types of

5

investments of power exist, what ends they serve and the consequences that arrive from them. They are not mutually exclusive, and as Foucault points out, 'in history you can find a lot of examples of these three kinds of social struggles, either isolated from each other, or mixed together. But even when they are mixed, one of them, most of the time, prevails' (Foucault 1983a: 212). The subject wants to meet the visual on his/her own terms, regardless of whether they like it or dislike it.

In his essay on *Governmentality*, Foucault talks about the art of government with reference to Machiavelli's *The Prince* (1515). By working through Machiavelli's writings, Foucault analyses the art of government and its objective concerning the exercising of power. Briefly, Foucault looks at the relation of power of the Prince and his principality, and seeks to analyse the link between them from the perspective of how they are joined as well as how they are separated. The Prince is located at a distance from his principality despite his control and integral association with it. The principality concurrently defines and excludes the position of the Prince as well as the person of the Prince, even though the principality may have been gained through conquest or legacy. This link between the Prince and his principality is what is at risk in this power relation, as the Prince needs to be constantly vigilant in the manner of protecting, serving and strengthening his people. The exercising of power in terms of the Prince and the principality is not 'to reinforce, strengthen and protect' (Foucault 2002: 204) the people but rather is more concerned with preserving the position of the Prince.

Relating this back to visual cultures, the image functions in the similar position of the Prince and the governed individual as the principality. The link between the image and governed individual is constantly under threat from other spectating subjects (the 'Prince's enemies') who may interfere with any form of visual social domination, through presenting knowledge that may challenge the dominance of the image. Other threats that may subvert the image are other visuals that have stronger seductive qualities. What the image seeks to protect is not the governed individual but more the concept of governing the individual – a protection of Kant's fondness for the state. This is what the Prince achieves; in protecting his principality, he protects his position as Prince and maintains management and control, as well as separating himself from what he produces – a well-defined, well-ordered principality.[2]

The position of the Prince can also be viewed from the place of the spectating subject. Here the spectating subject functions in the position of the Prince and forms their investment of power on a similar basis as the Prince's protection of his people. As the principality is isolated from but still connected to the Prince, so is the spectating subject isolated from their criticality with regards to the image and visual cultures. In refusing to become governed by the social dominance of the visual, the spectating subject forms an isolated position, as such a refusal distances the image from the spectating subject. Through this liberation from a visual economy that manages individuals, the spectating subject exercises a form of power, at a cost. To refuse a specific site reinforces the link between the image and governed individual as much as it reinforces the lack of a link between a governed individual and spectating subject. The spectating subject produces a questioning position in order to escape a governed viewing position, yet in doing so is kept distant from the visual as a consequence.

SUBJECTION

Foucault's 'form of power' enables us to discuss the subject that exists within an identico-centric realm, as the type of power that we are looking at, and critiquing, is a power that is completely focused on the birth of the subject from governed individual. The power struggles not only help to establish and consolidate a sense of subjectivity, they wrestle with any order that assists the government of the individual. Foucault states that using the term 'to govern, in this sense, is to structure the possible field of actions of others' (Foucault 1983a: 221). Relating this to visual cultures, we can use Foucault's notion of power to mark the shift in subjectivity from an uncritical and unaware spectating position to a conscious and self-reflexive positioning with respect to an image.

The institution of the image designates specific spectating positions from which the subject is required to view the image in order to obtain its 'proper' meaning[3] (this forms part of the privilege of knowledge that the governed individual must struggle against in order to become a critical spectating subject). This power relies on a communication of strict systematic signification and/or symbolization. This typology of information that comes from the image is not to be ignored in looking at the function of power, and indeed isn't by the subject, yet it is to be separated not from what is happening within the spectating subject, but between the spectating subject and the image. Because we are looking at power as a relational force, its existence is not completely dependent on systems of signification and can't be read primarily within such a frame. This would suppose that power pre-exists a relationship, which it does not. To define power relationships only within a communicative domain is to restrict their importance and effect for the subject, as it presents the subject–image connection as given and definitive.

To separate this classification of power relations from others is not to negate them but rather to extend power's effect and function particularly between the image and the subject. Indeed Foucault asserts that there are three types of relationship involved when power is exercised and it is important even when focusing on one of these, more than the others, to be aware that it is their interrelationship that ultimately determines a comprehensive analysis of power relations. By doing this we are not limited to viewing *how* power is invested in the image but can also include *why* and *what the consequences are* as a result of such an investment.

Kant and Foucault: investing the power

The power relations present in visual cultures that we are interested in exist outside systems of communication but also rest alongside them. In the moment of resistance to the form of power (or what Foucault terms the totalizing of the individual) the spectating subject asks the question 'What are we?' The subject shifts from a relationship of power based on communication and signification, and gravitates towards producing and defining meanings in relation to image from a position of self. In his article 'The Subject and Power' (Foucault 1983a), Foucault talks of Kant's paper that discusses the question 'What is the Enlightenment?' This is, for Foucault, part of the issue of the Enlightenment – that is, the formation of a type of subjectivity. In engaging with this question, Kant's paper also asks a more fundamental question for any subject (spectating or otherwise), 'What are we?', that being a critical inquiry into the current status of the individual – the first step towards refusing and struggling against the government of individualization. 'When in 1784 Kant asked "What is the Enlightenment?" he meant, "what is going on just now? What is happening to us? What is this world, this period, this precise moment in which we are living?" Or in other words: What are we, as *Aufklärer*, as part of the Enlightenment? … But Kant asks something else: What are we? In a very precise moment of history. Kant's question appears as an analysis of both us and our present' (Foucault 1983a: 216). This question 'What are we?' does more than merely direct focus to the subject and their position within a current socio-historical domain, rather it demands that the subject adopts a critical perspective of themselves, their function and being to live out an active existence.

For Kant, the individual is responsible for his or her own tutelage, and the escape from it must also be self-incurred. The change from governed individual to spectating subject must be a responsibility of the individual, and the subject asking the question 'What are we?' instigates this shifting process from a passive to active subjectivity. This question is where the investment of power occurs. On the precipice of where both subject and image define and position themselves, where the struggles are fought with respect to a configuration of an individual's subjectivity, the power relation is also an investment of power. The individual asking 'What are we?' emphasizes a conscious self-reflexive moment that signals the investment of power in the image for a subject. It marks the shift from subject to spectating subject, and for him/her, redefines how all images are viewed. 'What are we?' not only engages with struggles and power relations, it also identifies and concurrently resists the seduction of the state. Both Foucault and Kant acknowledge that the subject has a fondness for the state; the seduction to live out an uncritical and unquestioning existence forms part of the attraction of any image.

When we gaze at the image we enter into a multitude of relations, forming an investment of power. This is most critical as it fundamentally positions the subject and the image, individually and with respect to one another, and aims to classify each through an exercising of power. The power relation is played out on the threshold of the subject's gaze and the gaze of the image.

The image: the invitation

Each time an image is looked at, the image re-asks itself 'What are we?' and rotates in a constant cycle of liminal questioning. The image asks this question as it seeks to totalize the individual. In asking 'What are we?' from its position as image, it is determining the position from which it is to be viewed. It is important to note that the image asks this question to define a position but still recognizes the freedom of the subject. Once a subject has entered into a discourse with the image, the image possesses the privilege of knowledge and uses it in its exercising of power to the best effect possible. If we take as an example a piece of art like Andy Warhol's *Four Marilyns*,[c] and compare it to another such as Diego Velázquez's *The Rokeby Venus*,[d] we have two images that, superficially, seem to stand at diametric ends of a visual cultural spectrum. Both paintings hang in veritable institutions-as-state, London's National Gallery (Velázquez) and Warhol's versions of Monroe are to be found in similar institutions including the Tate Gallery, and yet his series of images is culturally set up to be read as holding a different position within the art world. The Warhol image of the four Marilyns represents the genre of contemporary art, generically subverting the entire concept of representation and the image, at the same time as deconstructing the myth of celebrity, through repeatedly presenting its representation. Velázquez's painting draws on classical mythology and represents Venus, the goddess and personification of beauty and all that is feminine, with her son Cupid. Here Venus looks not only at herself but also seems to look at the viewer. The image that is reflected in the mirror is ambiguous due to its opacity. This opacity is part of the idea that it exists in a different realm of mirrors and *mirrorness*, like the non-real world that we often find in the Baroque. Each image, provocative in its own way, deals with the question of femininity and its representation through looking at their place and function within a phallo-socio-centric context. The power relation from a spectator's perspective brings them much closer together, as here the paintings operate under similar surveillance despite their distance. *The Rokeby Venus* comes from a recognized canonical position within the art world, appearing to oppose Warhol's piece despite its similar reverence as canonical art.

The subject: the refusal

In order to become a spectating subject, making conscious identification with images, the subject also needs to ask 'What are we?' The subject asks it from a different point of view as this inquiry is a refusal. It asks only to say 'I am not', but the 'I am not' is in response to the determining position asked by the image. In the Louvre sits da Vinci's *Mona Lisa*.[e] It is an attraction of the museum, one of its treasures, and yet when you enter the room the painting is encased behind glass and seems very small in comparison with the many other paintings in the room. Why does the *Mona Lisa* attract the crowd? Because it is the best painted? Because it is the most aesthetically pleasing? Or because, as an image, the *Mona Lisa* is a culturally recognized 'piece of art'? As a highly valued object of art, the *Mona Lisa* reflects the history of art and the art gallery as institution-as-state. Here, the power exercised by the image invokes a desire within the subject to become a part of the body and privilege of knowledge within the image. The subject has choices in its meeting with the image and in its asking of the subjectivity defining the question 'What are we?' Its subjectivity can be invested in the image, within the confines of the image so that the governed individual remains controlled but within the discourse of the image. The subject is not only seduced by the image but also by the state. Viewing the *Mona Lisa* becomes

9

more about the act of viewing and being included in a cultural moment rather than viewing the *Mona Lisa* as a singular piece of (dare we say it) everyday art.

THIS IS NOT A BODY: POWERFUL AND SICK BODIES

Continuing on from the previous section, our main focus will be to conceptualize these Foucauldian forms of power, and power struggles, to the more image-specific example of the body. Given that our culture is saturated with a diverse range of bodies from the canonical to the popular to the sub-cultural, our example keeps the issue of representation of the body[4] separate from the topic at hand. That is to track the investment of power in the image via the body, through forms of visual media; the body as resemblance and as similitude; and to argue visual cultures as responsible for our culturally constructed corporality. In using the body as an example of an investment of power from a spectating subject, we can develop the concept of power relations working as discursive practice in visual cultures, subsequently arguing that all images, specifically here bodies, are interpreted through forms of power.

This section looks at the construction of corporal representation in visual culture rather than the topographical interpretation of the heterogeneity of bodies, and involves the spectator at the primary level of thinking about the formation of the visual. By looking closely at how bodies are formed through a framework of power, we include the spectator from the start, but more importantly, trace the spectator's transformation from governed individual to spectating subject. By not focusing on exclusive representations of the body, we free ourselves from the confines of genre and visual mediums, and can look at typologies of the body and how they function in terms of investing power, and power as a discursive practice. The aim is to use representations of the body for the reasons they were created – to create a spectator that responds and invests their subjectivity into the visual through a power structure. It is not just a response and/or investment to any representation of the body but a response/investment to all bodies, disruptive bodies, sick bodies, healthy bodies, attractive bodies, feminine bodies, black bodies, Asian bodies, masculine bodies, Caucasian bodies, infantile bodies, bodies that tear, bodies that mend, bodies that move, that stand still, and so on. What are the effects of such investments of power that occur here in order to produce a spectating subject? Keeping with the example of the body, do different representations of the body construct different spectating positions? Looking at examples of particular constructions of imaged bodies can help us deal with these sorts of questions.

Powerful bodies

For Foucault, power is produced, managed and organized by various socio-cultural discourses, some of his most famous examples being the discourses of medicine and sexuality operating as institutions. In examining these discourses, Foucault is analysing the actions that happen on the individual, noting what power relations are constructed as a result of these actions. In *Discipline and Punish* (1987) Foucault explains the spectacle of public execution, and uses it to exemplify how power relations are established and controlled through the state or government as institution, and how this governmentality and state control within culture and society is acted out on the body through modes of punishment.

In his analysis of tortured territory (concerning both body and culture) Foucault uses the body as a corporal example, for his new configurations of power and power-knowledge. The body works as power's tangible reality and active existence, as from this perspective, this is what power (and power-knowledge, to which we will return later) enters into and becomes for Foucault. After creating a visual sense of the condemned body, we are taken to the spectacle of the scaffold – where the body is put on display as an example for other bodies, and tortured. The body is a fundamental part of Foucault's larger research objective – the genealogy of the human being becoming a subject and how systems of knowledge and power produce each other, their manifestations acted out through visual constructions of the body.

These manifestations produce social orders of the body, as different power structures and relations are imbued with different knowledges. The implications of knowledge in this regard are the typologies of discursive practices that form multiple interpreting positions. Foucault suggests that we discard the separation of power and knowledge as forms that exist outside of and separate to each other, and instead view power and knowledge as inextricably linked, symbiotic forces that produce and propel each other through respective connotations:

> power produces knowledge ... power and knowledge directly imply one another; that there is no power relation without the correlative constitution of a field of knowledge, nor any knowledge that does not presuppose and constitute at the same time power relations. These 'power-knowledge relations' are to be analysed, therefore, not on the basis of a subject of knowledge who is or is not free in relation to the power system, but, on the contrary, the subject who knows, the objects to be known and the modalities of knowledge must be regarded as so many effects of these fundamental implications of power-knowledge and their historical transformations.
>
> (Foucault 1987: 27–8)

Foucault's clever neologism 'power-knowledge' has little direct connection with the image or visual culture, but through tracking its currency borne from construction and its development and activity in multiple discourses, it is possible to apply it to visual cultures. What this means for the spectator is that they meet the visual image with a prior corpus of knowledge, an archive of varying images ready to be drawn upon in any visual culture, producing a typology of knowledge based on the visual image they find. For the spectator, it is the power-knowledge combination of power struggles and relations that have constructed the visual image in question, and that controls and governs the knowledges and discursive practices that are invested in. This is how one body can generate more than one discourse in the social order. The body becomes a supportive structure for relations of power and knowledge allowing the spectating subject to invest in the corporal image and subjugate it through transforming the image into an object of knowledge. A filmic example of this is found in *Lord of the Rings: The Fellowship of the Ring* (Jackson 2001). Gandalf increases his size and presence (in response to Bilbo's procrastination regarding the letting go of the ring) to emphasize his capacity and greatness as a wizard, whereas in the second *Lord of the Rings: The Two Towers* (Jackson 2002) Gollum, as a filthy little creature, has a small, grey body, contorted and shrivelled reflecting his ideologies, who he is and what he invests in. Yet when he allows his repressed identity, Sméagol, more control over his mind, his eyes become wider, mimicking honesty and sincerity. They are more childlike, demonstrating the idea that it was his innocence and naivety that brought him to this state, rather than any overwhelming greed. We visually observe these same qualities in Frodo, and can foresee a similar fate. For the governed individual, relations of power and knowledge imposed on the visual image are seductive and the subject is the one who is subjugated and objectified.

Such heterogeneity helps to frame the body to be read differently from other bodies, similar bodies and, at times, in contrast to the same body. In the television series *Buffy the Vampire Slayer*, Buffy's sexualized body is different from Buffy's active, fighting body because their separate actions outlay the social orders of the same body. Buffy as lover/girlfriend calls for an investment from the spectator in the power relations that recognize the body of the feminine, the vulnerable[5] and the object of affection. The spectator, to invest in the discourse of love, reads the costumes and hairstyles on the body of Buffy's body-as-girlfriend, as well as her bodily actions. The same textual components symbolize a different social order of Buffy's body when she begins to slay. Buffy-as-slayer/saviour body draws on connotations of decisiveness, combat, assertion – not usually found in the discourse of love. Certain things such as costume, make-up, setting, and so on, foreground the discourse and become conventionalizing signifiers so that the spectator can invest in a specific power structure. Through investing in the power-knowledge of Buffy's body and, concurrently, bodies on television, the spectator understands that Buffy's body hasn't changed, but has in the sense that it has transformed and moved across discourses. Buffy-as-girlfriend (or sex symbol) operates via an alternate set of actions to that of Buffy-as-slayer. The corporal signifier of Buffy is constant but the surrounding signs and relations of power have altered as a result of how her body is imaged and constructed in shifting discourses.[6]

Using Foucault's example of the spectacle, we can look at these social orders of the body as the spectacle, the body itself as spectacle, and the spectacle of the body, to see how the construction of the body image is riddled with actions of power. The aim is not to methodically work through the multiple representations of the body in varying discourses to see how they are powerful in their own right, or to see how a body works within specific social orders, but rather to employ the social orders of the body to exemplify how an image, as part of a visual culture, is constructed for a specific action. Buffy possesses a sense of meta-corporeality in that it is her super-strength that not only forms part of the thematic and narrative core of the programme but also provides secondary material for each episode. Each episodic instalment adds to strengthen Buffy both as vampire slayer but also Buffy as helpless female. Every demon and vampire that she fights and every problem that she solves (with the assistance of her gang) offsets her vulnerability in relationships with cast members. Buffy's body is not purely 'a body' in this television programme; it becomes a vessel that carries the issues, morals and problematic of the script through its narrative. In terms of the spectacle, Buffy corporealizes the torture exacerbated by power relations. Her torture is emotional and physical. Action in this sense referring to Foucault's reworking of power as a social feature that holds currency only once 'it is put into action' Foucault (1983a: 219), and in terms of power relations possessing a discursive function. This is not to deny that representations of the body will play an important and central part in such a study of the constructed corporal image, as some discussion will be necessary in order to observe how a social order of the body is constructed and how such a construction of the imaged body affects the spectating subject.

Sick bodies

To look at the body and power requires an understanding of the fragmentary nature of the representation of the body, as each representation is made meaningful and accessible via the discourse through which it is interpreted. Looking at a cinematic image of the body, in *Pulp Fiction* (Tarantino 1994) the sick body of Mia Wallace functions differently to the sick body of Andrew Beckett in *Philadelphia* (Demme 1993) – the display of the body is read through and, subsequently, enforces and strengthens the power of the discourse in which it appears. Both operate on the basis of the spectacle, as the body becomes the site for investment of power and its related, supportive structures of control and knowledge. The following bodies symbolize how the spectacle is a foundation for the intersection of investments from the spectator. As the spectator watches the imaged body, the process of interpretation is bound up with discourses of resistance. The narrative importance and development of Mia Wallace's sick body is used to emphasize the film's transgressive quality, which deals with the inversion of the dominant social order, in terms of race, sexuality and mortality. Her body is the spectacle as it embraces the structural dissolution of the power-knowledge of the normalized and institutionalized body in the social order. This is how her overdose is viewed as Rabelaisian, becoming humorous instead of incredibly tragic. The social order of Mia's body is used as a double synecdoche, first for the transgressive discourse of the film, and second for all bodies that oppose the homogeneous social order opposed in this film, in this way.

In *Pulp Fiction*, Mia's sick body is treated with humour, the threat of her death bearing more importance on Vincent's moral promise to his employer, rather than any breaking of the social law. Saving Vincent's own mortality is given as the primary reason to save Mia's life rather than any desire to rescue Mia's of her drug taking and an interest to put her on the 'right track'. This interpretative framing of Mia's sick body prepares the spectating

13

subject for the death of Marvin in the back of Jules's car to treat it with the same humour, further emphasizing the transgressive socio-cultural order and ensuing power relations that are present within the film. In *Philadelphia*, Andrew Beckett's sick body functions differently. Here is a sick body that also, in Foucauldian terms, works as a spectacle. The body is used as a vessel to carry and draw attention to the power relations at work in the social reality and order of the film. Andrew's illness, AIDS, embodies the sickness of homophobia in the social order far more than the homophobic lawyer that he pays to represent him. The representation of his AIDS-ridden body is constructed to specify the position of gay bodies to the hegemonic social institutions in culture. Andrew's sickness is not humorous and it doesn't signify any transgressive element in the film but it does personify the marginalization of homosexuals, and any respective 'transgressive' representation within the cultural order outside of the image.

The character of I in *Withnail and I* (Robinson 1987) exemplifies a similar social order of the body as spectacle and the spectacle as body, and also deals with the corporal abjection of such narrative transgression. I functions as Withnail's foil, inoffensive, unworldly and dispassionate to Withnail's irrepressible debauchery, their bodies both representing their inability to function in a normal world. They both approach the washing-up as tacticians of germ warfare. Withnail embodies the body as spectacle through his dramatic prose, extreme drug taking and abuse on the physicality of the body – although this is part of the spectacle of the body as Withnail's social immoderation concentrates the intersection of control and power on the body (Withnail, wearing underpants and muscle rub, swallows lighter fluid in defiance to I (who acts here as the enforcement of the symbolic order) and promptly vomits). Their abjection locates their bodies just outside the cultural order forcing the abject body to be easily seen as constructed due to its fragile placing in relations of power.

> The abject has only one quality of the object – that of being opposed to I. If the object, however, through its opposition, settles me within the fragile texture of a desire for meaning, which, as a matter of fact, makes me ceaselessly and infinitely homologous to it, what is abject on the contrary, the jettisoned object, is radically excluded and draws me toward the place where meaning collapses.
>
> (Kristeva 1982: 2)

We deal with abjection and the body in much greater depth in the Kristeva chapter, so for the moment this issue is held in readiness.

Investing power in the imaged body

Much of Foucault's work deals with the body and its significance to the social order and cultural *zeitgeist*. His work in *Discipline and Punish: The Birth of the Prison* (1987) is helpful in looking at the construction of power-infused visual cultures. Specifically, Foucault's spectacle is that of the public execution and the scaffold – the physical apparatus that supports a public execution. Foucault's work is concerned with the 'body' of the scaffold, looking both at the 'body' of public execution as a spectacle and as a separate action/discourse of power relations. He also addresses the 'body' of the people versus the state, examining how public execution itself became a scaffold for the power relations between the victims, the guilty, the innocent and the government of the state. Foucault uses the scaffold as spectacle to establish the public execution as an example of how investments of power are formed through structures that enforce a social order. His example of the tortured prisoner is used to highlight, in a vulgar manner, how social and cultural order was maintained through a public exercising of state power: 'it is largely as a force of production that the body is invested with relations of power and domination; but, on the other hand, its system of subjection (in which need is also a political instrument meticulously prepared, calculated and used); the body becomes a useful force only if it is both a productive body and a subjected body' (Foucault 1987: 26).

Foucault uses this term 'body' to exact the connotations of what is known and familiar, as well as that which is unseen. His double use of the term body lets us look at the wider picture of how any idea attached to and of the body itself is one that is formed through a series of relations of power. How we view bodies as physical beings, or in Foucault's example, as dead bodies walking, depends on the investments of power that are formed in the 'body' of discourses that contain these visualized bodies. In order to assess and critique how the body is a constructed image, we need to look more closely at how it is caught up in a 'system of subjection'.

Foucault talks of a political technology of the body, which is a term he coins to denote that 'there may be a "knowledge" of the body that is not exactly the science of its functioning, and a mastery of its forces that is more than the ability to conquer them' (Foucault 1987: 26). This knowledge exists prior to the body; that is, various institutions frame our bodies before they are *our* bodies. It is this interplay between the body as institutionalized knowledge and its propensity of resisting such forces that occupy Foucault for much of his intellectual (and perhaps personal) life. In this sense when we speak about the Foucauldian body it is as much an intellectual pursuit as it is a personal one. No body exists prior to an investment of power, the investment of power is already made. Reading power relations as forms of investment in this way hints at their capacity to become submissive as well as resistant investments.

A 'knowledge' of the body that is not exactly the science of its functioning suggests an awareness of the limit of one's own corporality compared to another's. A beyondness to the body with regards to both its corporality and corporeality[7] is what Foucault is referring to when he talks of 'a mastery of forces that is more than the ability to conquer them'. The discourse of medicine is a good example as all bodies and bodily actions are already read before medical practitioners see them. Medicine positions the body in a very specific manner for this is the basis of what it terms 'treatment'. Foucault's *The Birth of the Clinic: An*

Archaeology of Medical Perception (1975) demonstrates how the history of medicine is in fact a history of the positioning of the body in terms of disease, health, decrepitude and well-being. The body through medicine is constantly framed, constructed and placed. Actions of power (the investment either through resistance or through subjection) within the discursive practice of medicine operate in the structure of a hyper social order.[8] The normal appears more normal, the sane appear saner, the sick more sick, the crazy more crazy, and so on. An interesting example of this can be found in *Girl, Interrupted* (Mangold 1999).

In this film, Susanna's body is positioned in a certain way. She signs herself in to the psychiatric hospital, Claymoore, but cannot sign herself out. This is the investment of power here as we read the image of Susanna's body through the discourses of the sick, the insane and the actions of the other bodies in the film. The 'I sign myself in I sign myself out' illustrates that Susanna no longer has power over her body, not until the institution (Claymoore) agrees that her control over and of her body is in compliance with their own ideal.[9] Lisa, on the other hand, embodies the physicality of the women in the institution and the potential for resistance within such a system of subjection. Lisa forms a central part of what Claymoore stands for – rehabilitation and reassimilation into society – but at the same time acts out the corporal dysfunction within the regime. Lisa wants to be free, but seeks her freedom within the scope of Claymoore's hyper social order. As a result, her rebellion is a response to the institution and by resisting its normalizing discourse (refusing to take prescribed medication, escaping) and its desensitizing processes; Lisa's body becomes a superficial manifestation of the exercising of power used to maintain social order. The prescribed drugs are a part of this exercise of power, controlling the threat of appearing to fit in the social order outside of Claymoore. Lisa also resists the sites of opposition to the institution.

Lisa represents the conundrum of the system of subjection as she resists the institution, like the spectating subject resists the prescribed viewing position, through running away and breaking its social order and laws. Yet she is drawn to it, she wants herself as well as her resistance to be acknowledged by it, hence she returns time and time again after her escapes. The other female characters represent other investments of power in the body image – the burnt body, the anorexic body, the fat body, and the body with ambiguous sexuality. As a unit these typologies of bodies join to produce a system of subjection and sustain it. The supposed sexual promiscuity of Susanna reflects the Foucauldian conception of a body framed by an institution. Susanna is not compulsively promiscuous (surely not based on an affair with an older man,[10] a frolic with her boyfriend and kissing an orderly) but the investment of power is to read her in this way.

Foucault corporealizes the creation of the visual. Opening two of his most famous works, *The Order of Things* and *Discipline and Punish* is the discussion of the visual over and of the body. There is never a sense of separation between the act of painting, the painter and the painting. Infused in all visual culture, is the notion of the body whether it is its absence, its consumption, its abjection or its seduction. Foucault begins his analysis of

Velázquez's *Las Meninas*[by describing in specific detail a picture that encompasses not only the form and content of the painting but the actual corporeal act of painting and the painter himself. This configuration becomes his critical drive in looking at the painting. Using this format, we can look at how power relations and the body work with and against each other through some visual examples.

Constructed senses

One way to extend these discussed notions of investments and relations of power and knowledge, and their relevance to image is to deconstruct the body, allowing a focus to develop on random features of the body to emphasize how actions on the body, particularly within visual cultures, symbolize the body's construction and the relative actions that exist outside the body but are connected to it either through narrative importance, socio-historical or socio-cultural significance. This is intended to highlight how imaged elements of corporeality form discursive practices and how power relations are read through them.

BLOOD

Blood is used as a signifier to symbolize a range of bodily existences – life, impending death, death, and so on. There are different colours of blood, from the bright red in *The Shining* (Kubrick 1980), to the dark opaque ruby in *Blood Simple* (Coen Brothers 1984), to the glossy marron red in *ER*, to acid blood in all the *Alien* films and silvery fluid for blood in *Terminator 2* (Cameron 1991), and even to the absence of blood – the spectrum of colour symbolizing the spectrum of various bloody situations a body can be located within. In *The Shining*, the blood flowing from the elevator denotes life that was once present and lost, the blood linking previous bodies in the Overlook Hotel to the present ones. The blood links the previous caretaker, Mr Grady, with his family murders and the follow-on effect of terror is a result of the blood signifying this domain of knowledge – an acknowledgement of the conventions within the horror genre, the past murders, and Jack's re-enactment of the past events at the Overlook Hotel. The blood itself does not produce the knowledge of terror or a similar investment from the spectator, rather it is the power-knowledge (made up in part of the struggles of forms of power that were discussed at the beginning of this chapter) and of what blood signifies within this particular discourse that rests *on top* of the image and outlines the potential fields for meaning within this visual image.

The blood in *ER* forms part of the programme's realist aesthetic, which is far removed from the horror blood used in *The Shining*. First, the quantity of blood is dramatically reduced, and its signifying parameters have been altered to produce a positive response (and illicit a like investment) from the spectator. Blood in this visual example is used as an element of life – something sustains it and improves the chance of survival, whereas the blood in *The Shining* is used to denote the threat of life loss. Both bloods are abject to the spectating subject as it represents the fragility and liminality of the body but also the fragility of the imaged body. The blood is not real but its reality effect[11] is so forceful and compelling that the investment of power in such an image and its signification, makes it seem very real for the spectator – such as the splatter of blood and bits of Private Pile's brain hitting the tiled bathroom wall after he shoots himself through the mouth, in *Full Metal Jacket* (Kubrick 1987).

TEETH

Just as part of blood's image serves to contribute to the classification of genre and its coding, teeth order and stress the discursive practices through which the spectator must read the image. In *The Mask* (1994), Jim Carrey's teeth follow his metamorphosis from a quiet, unassuming masculinity to a verbose, gregarious masculinity. As the Mask gets louder, his teeth get bigger, as do his eyes and other body parts. The connotative importance of growing teeth is that their size is symbolizing the empowerment of Stanley Ipkiss. The teeth become more than a prominent facial feature, they represent Ipkiss's low self-esteem and crisis of confidence. For Ipkiss power is found being comfortable in social situations, with beautiful women and standing up to confrontation. The Mask is both displaying Ipkiss's discomfort and inability to remain calm in these situations and how to act in an extrovert way would be like putting on a different costume – or a larger set of teeth.

In *Jaws* (Spielberg 1975), we have a whole fish that is represented through its teeth. The qualities of fear are channelled into the bite of the shark and the physical attack. The discursive practices of tension, panic, unknowing and isolation are heightened through the anticipation of seeing a shark fin – which works to unify all the shark's teeth so that we do not solely see the fin, but a large tooth slicing through the water. The fin operates as a synecdoche for the attack – the bite and subsequent feasting on the human body.

MUSCLES

The Acrobat's Exercises (1928), *Intermission* (1927/28), *Les Liaisons Dangereuses* (1926) and *Eternal Evidence* (1930)[8] are examples from Magritte's *oeuvre* which are very close thematically to the construction of both the corporeal image and the image in general. Magritte forces us to first connect the images in *Eternal Evidence*, only to re-dissect and re-order them arbitrarily. We read the images in the conventional Western way of interpretation – from top to bottom, left to right. The second frame of the woman's breasts, followed by the third frame of a vagina, compels the spectator to form an investment in the image – that we are looking at a cut-up picture of a woman, and that these pictures are of the same woman. Magritte's purposeful separation of bodily parts forces the spectator to invest in the construction of the body – in order to put it back together again – and then resist such an arbitrary construction by responding to the purposeful separation of the images. The body is presented as a fragmented work of art, assembled in the manner and laws of anatomical correctness. The separating frames undermine this hierarchy and, despite the closeness attempted through the nakedness of the body, we are kept at a distance because of it. There is nothing in this composition that tells us that the first frame of the face is a woman's, only the culturally learnt paradigm of reading an image, and a body, in this way makes us return to the top and state 'this [the painting, the face] is a woman'.

This distance from image and body (nakedness working as a fundamental part of this estrangement instead of its trying to create intimacy) is further illustrated in *Les Liaisons Dangereuses* (1926). The picture of the woman appears to be inverted, but on closer inspection, the woman is holding up a mirror. Foucault states, 'The mirror functions a little like a fluoroscope, but with a whole play of differences' (Foucault 1983a: 51) making clear the body is functioning as similitude.[12] Magritte, by painting a reflected body of a woman, comments not only on the construction of the image, but also on the construction of 'woman' in culture. The distance of the image from spectator, is heightened by this doubling of disintegration of the image and, particularly here, the female image in culture. Magritte's use of the mirrored body shows that the image fills a space within culture that is contrived and imagined. By making these two women 'unjoinable', Magritte struggles with and resists the power-knowledge that attempts to determine the imaged body as true reflection of the actual real human body.

FINGERNAILS

In *Twin Peaks* (Lynch), the murderer of Teresa Banks and Laura Palmer (and the attempted murder of Ronnette Polanski) places a piece of paper with an initial on it under their fingernails. Here we are presented with a non-corporeal substance embedded deep into the corporeal. The initial signifies the lack of meaning an image has on its own, and connects itself as well as the dead bodies with the narrative of the television programme. The initials from the girls' fingers turn out to spell the murderer's name – a further action on the body that only possesses meaning once it has been applied to discourses outside the body. The particular use of fingernails is interesting as the initial on the piece of paper has life in that it is a clue to the murder investigation. This piece of paper wedged underneath a dead person's fingernail tells more than the actual body itself.

In *CSI* we are presented with similar actions on the body. Here it is not so much the image of the body that cites investment of power from the spectator but the discourses of science and police that 'lift' meanings from the dead bodies. In one episode we are presented with a man that is found dead in the woods after a supposed hunting accident. The crime team collates evidence from the scene and also from the body. We are shown the passage of the bullet through the body, but only to further the scientific theories of how this man came to die. Death comes to define the imaged body as something that produces meanings on *top of it*, and in this sense there is beyondness to the body, as though it speaks from beyond the grave. This contextualization of the body is used to strengthen the governing discourses of science and law enforcement, which, when combined, produce a discourse of truth. This is why when we are left with a 'case unsolved' we are left feeling dissatisfied, as though this discourse of truth has lost some of its power-knowledge.

These singled-out parts/aspects of the body are not exhaustive but are intended to illustrate the various discourses that the body appears in to different ends.

Notes

1 The term 'spectating subject' is used to distinguish between a passive and active subjectivity. In order to effectively use power as a tool to understand more about the subject's interaction with the image, a strict focus on the actions of the subject is required, especially as we are setting up a power relationship between image and subject.

2 This is similar to Kant's notion of the realm of obedience and its distinction from the realm of use of reason in light of the struggle of exploitation. Self-incurred tutelage is what exploits the individual. To escape it requires distinction between obedience and reason. If this struggle of exploitation separates the individual from what he or she produces, then escaping one's own tutelage is also self-produced. A negotiation of obedience and reason produced by the subject exploits the tutelage and distances the subject from it.

3 Part of the subject's resistance to this government of individualization is to recognize the institution's designated spectating position so that there is something to resist against. More later in chapter.

4 We refer the reader to the text *New Developments in Film Theory* (Fuery 2000), which looks at the representation of the body in cinema via Foucault's (and other theoreticians') work.

5 To avoid the sense of phallocentric bias – the vulnerability mentioned is used to signal the vulnerability found in love not found in a woman in love.

6 See also Chapter 2, 'Seeing the self in the Baroque mirror: Lacan and the visual', for a different discussion of Lacan's third time.

7 The distinction made here is to separate the body's physicality with its metaphysical presence and conceptions.

8 See Chapter 6, 'Invisibility and hallucination: the state of the image in the postmodern world', for a deeper discussion on the issue of the hyper.

9 The image of Winona Ryder in court for shoplifting from the Beverly Hills Saks store is the same sort of image we get of Susanna in this Foucauldian frame.

10 This raises the interesting point of how Susanna is deemed more promiscuous because she slept with a married man rather than any condemnation of the sexual and moral ethics of the man. In this way, not only is sexuality part of the system of subjection but a feminine sexuality.

11 See more on this in Chapter 5, 'Spectator, culture, image: Barthes and the visual'.

12 See Chapter 6, 'Invisibility and hallucination: the state of the image in the postmodern world', where there is a deeper discussion of similitude and Baudrillard.

a For some general examples of Renaissance art by the artists mentioned (Crivelli, Botticelli, Tura and Mantegna), please view the hyperlinks below.

Crivelli
http://www.kfki.hu/~arthp/html/c/crivelli/carlo/index.html
Botticelli
http://www.artchive.com/artchive/B/botticelli.html
Mantegna
http://www.kfki.hu/~arthp/html/m/mantegna
Tura
http://www.artcyclopedia.com/artists/tura_cosme.html

b Dali, *Christ of St John of the Cross*
http://dali.urvas.lt//page24.html

c Warhol, *Four Marilyns*
http://www.uol.com.br/23bienal/especial/iewa01g.htm

d   Velázquez, *The Rokeby Venus*
    http://www.nationalgallery.org.uk/cgi-
    bin/WebObjects.dll/CollectionPublisher.woa/wa/work?workNumber=NG2057

e   da Vinci, *Mona Lisa*
    http://www.louvre.fr/anglais/collec/peint/inv0779/peint_f.htm

f   Velázquez, *Las Meninas*
    http://www.artchive.com/meninas.htm

Unfortunately not all of the Magritte paintings discussed in this chapter are available for public viewing on the internet but the URLs below do offer information about the paintings and how to acquire the images should you wish to view them.

g   Magritte
    http://www.masterpiece-paintings-gallery.com/rene-magritte-1.htm
    http://www.magritte.com/
    This website offers some selected images of Magritte for public viewing:
    http://www.artchive.com/artchive/M/magritte.html
    The Treachery of Images
    http://www.the-artfile.com/uk/artists/magritte/pipe.htm

Other artworks
http://www.the-artfile.com/uk/gallery/magritte.htm

Chapter Two

SEEING THE SELF IN THE ☐ BAROQUE MIRROR

Lacan and the visual

Perhaps men would have to learn everything anew, and especially how to read an image.

(Lacan 1988b: 47)

The metaphoricity of the mirror

Jacques Lacan, perhaps the one who was more Freudian than Freud himself, loved the mirror. Even in his old age he was known to be unable to resist stolen glances of himself as he walked by a mirror. And why not? For here was the man who spent his intellectual life holding up the speculum to the unconscious and, in the process, to the social order of things. For Lacan, the mirror was both an intellectual pursuit and a personal obsession, it was an instrument of analysis and a process of forming subjectivities. Lacanian theory depends on the mirror in part because it is a reminder of all the travails of what it is to exist. It is the mirror that marks the point at which we become the split, fragmented subject, torn from the ego-centric and the sense of the whole and placed into the realm of the signifier, that is the Symbolic. Psychoanalysis also depends on the mirror because here is an instrument invested in the visual – an issue at the core of this analytic process. In *The Four Fundamental Concepts of Psychoanalysis*, Lacan urges us to meditate on optics;[1] a sentiment we find in countless places in Freud, some of which we shall have reason to visit here. And, finally, Lacan's psychoanalytic methods depend on the mirror because of its metaphoricity. This is the mirror as it enables critical metaphors for some of the fundamental issues of psychoanalytic concerns. We will have more to say of Lacan's theory of, and relationship to, the mirror in a moment – but for now let us pursue a less declared aspect of Lacanian theory and style. This is an aspect that is as much about the style of Lacanian psychoanalysis as it is about the substance – and this includes the theme of the mirror and the visual. Here we encounter the idea that there is something altogether Baroque about Lacan and his works and ideas.

Hidden away in a seminar delivered towards the end of Lacan's life we find a few references to the Baroque. They would seem almost inconsequential, especially compared to the wealth of influences and forces of Surrealism found in Lacan's personal and professional life and works. Of course the surrealist allusions and connections make sense – from an early age he lived and socialized with key members of the surrealist movement. For example, Bataille was both a friend and a creative influence for Lacan; Salvador Dali and Lacan travelled in New York together. And yet there is something to be said for seeing Lacan, and his works, as a version of the Baroque rather than that of surrealism. As Lacan himself puts it: 'Comme quelqu'un l'a perçu réje me range – qui me range? Est-ce que c'est lui ou est-ce que c'est moi? Finesse de lalangue – je me range plutôt du côté du Baroque' Lacan 1975b: 97). (As someone recently noticed, I am situated/I situate myself – who situates me? Is it him or is it me? That is a subtlety of *lalangue* – I am situated/I situate myself on the whole on the side of the Baroque.) Lacan does not want to theorize the Baroque, or just use it for examples (although both of these become an inevitable part of the process), rather there is something altogether more subtle, more intriguing, developing here. One of the aspects is that his style, and so some of his ways of arguing, becomes an echo of it. To read/hear Lacan is to enter into a discourse of the Baroque. (The neologism we see in the above quotation – *lalangue* – is a good example of Lacan's baroque style. It is a word with a flourish, a certain excess about it.) If this is the case what then are the implications for interpreting Lacan? And why the Baroque? Let's commence by considering some of the essential features of the Baroque, for from this we can begin to read Lacan in a new way.

To remind ourselves, the Baroque was a style that followed Mannerism (so around 1600) and lasted, influentially speaking, into the eighteenth century.[2] It was a counter-reformation, Catholic-driven style full of emotions and excesses. It was typified by the desire to stir unease and strong emotional responses in the spectator by representing (through both form and subject matter) the extremes of passion.[3] Passion itself was one of the primary issues of the Baroque period, for here is an era that is marked by Descartes' philosophical ideas on the passions of the soul. For the Baroque artist, passion was something that was not additional to the work, it was the work, and it was why the work should exist at all. This is why so much of the Baroque was seen as extreme, even raw, emotion. The painting or sculpture, building or garden, existed in order to show some aspect of passion, to express passion and, perhaps most significantly of all, to evoke passion within the spectator. In these terms it could be argued that what perspectivism did in the Renaissance, the evocation of the passions did in the Baroque. For these processes of representation became the ways in which the image positioned the spectator. Perspective and depth of field located the spectator in a special position in terms of the painting, offering a specific site from which to observe the image. It set up a position in which we make sense of the image, creating a feeling of realism. Baroque can also be seen as locating the spectator, this time through the compulsion of passion – the spectator was to be swept up in the power and dynamism of the emotions on display. The Baroque would not hold back in this regard, and this is part of the reason why it has been seen as a style of excess.

Perhaps the two most famous artists of the formative period of the Baroque are Bernini and Caravaggio. Between them these two have come to typify the high Baroque style, in particular as it breaks from the Mannerist traditions. Lacan's references to Bernini are not that surprising – in some ways his comments on *The Ecstasy of St Teresa*[a] form part of a long tradition that sees the statue in these excessive, and eroticized, terms. The history of the statue primes Lacan's reading of it (which we shall look at in a moment). But Caravaggio, along with other artists of the Baroque that we may want to include, will need to be treated in a more metaphorical manner if we are to pursue this interpretation of Lacan's style and conceptual process. In doing so we can extend the ways in which Lacan, and psychoanalysis in general, can be used in the analysis of the visual. To do so we can begin with considering Lacan's references to the Bernini statue.

The Ecstasy of St Teresa captures so many of the key elements of the Baroque. Apart from this idea of the passions of the soul (which we shall return to in a moment), Bernini's sculpture demonstrates how the Baroque engaged in the powerfully visual and emotionally excessive. St Teresa swoons in her ecstatic state about to be pierced by the arrow of God; part of her expression is thus one of anticipation. Yet this is also an expression that shows the pleasures and pains of such penetrations as if they are already taking place. This is a moment outside of time, of the present and future, of that which is and what is to be. Such temporal slippage is a recurring element in the Baroque, for it is the attempt to create intense emotional responses through the anticipation of what is to come – an anticipation that is devised to be created within the onlooker. Note, for example, Caravaggio's *The Conversion of St Paul*,[b] which conveys all of its tension and action in a moment that we, as spectators, anticipate. Similarly, in other Bernini sculptures we see the anticipation of death fused with an expression that can only be described as orgasmic. Once more in Bernini we find the merging of anticipation (of death, suffering, and indeed God) with sexual fulfilment and excess.

In this sense the figures within the Caravaggio painting and the Bernini sculptures mirror the spectator's own visual expectations through this anticipation. This is a curious process for it is marking a moment in time where the whole issue of the image has yet to take place. The Baroque recognizes that part of the heightening of tensions in the emotions and passions is more excessive than the moment (of death, orgasmic climax). Fear, one of the great themes of the Baroque, is best shown in the moment before the event takes place, when this raw emotion becomes something else. There is a certain irony here of course, for the image turns out not to be what it suggests it is, or perhaps even what we experience it as, and recall it to be. *The Conversion of St Paul* and *The Ecstasy of St Teresa* are images prior to the significance of the event. It is as if we as spectators have arrived too early, catching the most excessive moment, but not its realization. Rather than exclude the spectator, however, such a temporal shift actually has the effect of suturing them into the image and its emotions. It relies on the imagination and emotional response of the absence of the actual fulfilment. So, St Teresa remains constantly ecstatic, the horse's hoof hovers always above the prostrate figure of St Paul.

This technique of anticipation is one of the primary devices of horror films, and in these terms the emotive responses from the spectator can be described as Baroque in effect. As spectators we are never so emotionally responsive (so filled with fear, anxiety, and of course pleasure) as when we are in that moment building up to the terror. The most horrific moments are almost always those that build up to the act, rather than the act itself. Of course the version of terror in horror films relies precisely on a sense of pleasure attained through a version of excess (in this sense the excess of a particular emotion attached to fear). Kristeva's idea of *frayage/frayeur* is useful here. In her essay 'Ellipsis on dread and the specular seduction' (Kristeva 1986a) Kristeva plays with the two words; *frayage* is roughly translated as pathway, and *frayeur* (with no etymological link) is dread and fear. Kristeva blends the two in an analysis of how the spectator is seduced through the specular. The spectator of the Baroque and the horror film are similarly seduced through the pathway and into emotional excess. This is the terror of seduction, and the seduction of terror. It contains the fascination that we desire in all versions of horror images that are constructed for pleasure. And one of the key elements to all this is the time of anticipation, when the terror exists but has not been revealed.

This sense of time and anticipation is also to be found in Lacan's ideas on the unconscious, particularly in terms of pleasure and desire. Pleasurable anticipation is the foundation of so many textual orders, and the visual is certainly no exception. It does not even have to be a narrative-based process, although this is certainly one of the more readily apparent versions. Lacan's ideas are helpful here because they demonstrate an awareness of the impossibility of the usual constructions of time within the unconscious. Here we are referring not so much to Freud's idea that temporal relations in dreams are often shown in much the same way paintings have represented time, but rather that time itself becomes a difficulty to be negotiated.[4] In another way – and this is what really interests us here – Lacan argues that time actually constitutes a paradigm which allows us to see a difference between the Imaginary and the Symbolic, particularly as they are experienced through the processes of subjectivity. Let us consider the story of the three prisoners, for through this we can continue our sense of the Baroque.

The story of the three prisoners

Three prisoners are put to a test. One of them is to be freed, but as all three are equally deserving, it is not clear which one should benefit from this unique act of mercy. They are told – *Here are three white discs and two black ones. Each of you will have one of these discs attached to his back, and you are going to have to work out for yourself so as to be able to tell us which one you have been stuck with. Obviously there is no mirror, and it isn't in your interest to communicate, since all it needs is for one of you to have revealed to another what he has got on his back for him to gain by it.*

(Lacan 1988b: 287)

Lacan takes this story and explains how the prisoners might work out the solution, but the point is that it is not simply a test of logic (for both the prisoners and Lacan's audience), but an issue that depends on temporality. The solution to the problem resides precisely in the time it takes to solve it;[5] and the significance of this story lies in the time taken to solve the problem. This special temporal order – the moment of hesitation and inaction that is so fundamental to solving the puzzle – is designated by Lacan as a third moment/time (*temps*). It is one that develops 'in relation to a speculation on the reciprocity of the subjects' (Lacan 1988b: 288). In other words it is the special order of time where each prisoner must think like the other two, observe their position of subjectivity, in order to understand his own. It requires him to think and feel like another person.

This is the same sort of time we find in the Baroque and in certain types of genres that depend so much on extremes of responses, such as horror and thrillers – it is the moment before the emotional revelation that becomes the defining quality. Just as the Baroque is so often focused on the emotional excess prior to climax, so we find in horror films the most significant times are the build-up to the point of terror and threat, rather than its actual exposition. This is the meaningfulness of the third time, for contained within it is the need to see reciprocity. (Or, put another way, what is happening elsewhere, to someone else, is brought into the sense of the self.) This is the moment when the spectator encounters the ecstatic Baroque, the shadowy figure of Mother as she stalks into the bathroom as Marion showers in *Psycho* (Hitchcock 1960), and the playing out of the terror of in-betweenness and non-existence in *The Sixth Sense* (Shyamalan 1999). The specular and impassioned responses by the audience take place because they enter into the same sort of relationship to the protagonists (and images) as the one that the prisoners must have in order to solve the enigma of the discs. One of the prisoners may well be given his freedom (that is, solve the riddle) but it is only through a process of a particular type of time that this can take place. This is a time heavy with meaning and significance; it is a non-causal time because relationships formed within this are significant only to the future.

The specific inflections given to this idea of the third time by Lacan, and our re-reading here, means that we must see this experience as a beyond to mere audience identification. This is not just the spectator's sense of empathy or catharsis (although there is something of these involved) for this third time requires slippage from the Symbolic (the social world order) and a more direct manifestation of the Imaginary (that psychic realm dominated by the ego, and hence sense of the self). What we mean by this is that when such a sensation is taking place it can be said that the text has made an additional requirement of the spectator. Just as the prisoner must experience the problem of the discs from the subjectivity of the other two in order to solve the riddle, sometimes the spectator experiences the text in terms of a different sense of subjectivity. Now this difference is not an especially easy phenomenon to articulate and in some ways approaches the sorts of reading processes that are theorized by Barthes and Eco.[6] The relative successes and failures of an image to illicit such a response have nothing to do with the textual processes, but are connected to the relationship of the image to power. In the case of the three prisoners this is nothing less than freedom; the first to be able to imagine, and therefore 'see' the situation of the other two is the one who will gain his freedom. For the spectator of Bernini's St Teresa or Hitchcock's *Psycho* it is the sensation of religious ecstasy or filmic horror. This emphasis on the Imaginary (the reflexivity of the self to the self as well as the institutions containing and wielding power, including the text itself – for genre is a form of textual power) has a further connection with the Baroque, one that involves the mirroring of the spectator.

The reflecting image and the self

In the background they watch what is about to take place, reflecting the spectator's own act of expectancy. These are the figures, often dim lit and shadowy, we find in the Baroque images that are more than backdrops to the central piece. They function to send the gaze back into the image as well as to return that of the spectator. They are the ones who participate in the challenging of orders – of the looker and the looked at – and in doing so the essential features of image and spectator are themselves challenged. These are the images that contest the space between spectator and image because they resist the idea that our gaze flows towards the image and reads it in this uni-directional fashion. Instead the image itself gazes back at us.[7] This act of mirroring and challenge is what we find in Lacan's theory of the Mirror Stage as it marks the transition between the egocentric subject driven by the primary edict of pleasure to the realm of the Symbolic, which is that of social order and the signifier.[8] It is noteworthy that for Lacan the essential difference between the Imaginary and the Symbolic lies in the conception of the subject:

> There is an inertia in the Imaginary which we find making itself in the discourse of the subject, sowing discord in the discourse, making it such that I do not realize that when I mean someone well, I mean him ill, that when I love him, it is myself that I love, or when I think I love myself, it is precisely at this moment that I love an other. . . . The issue is to know whether the Symbolic exists as such, or whether the Symbolic is simply the fantasy of the second degree of the Imaginary coadaptations.
>
> (Lacan 1988b: 306–7, translation modified)

There are two key points here: first, that the Imaginary insists on an insertion of the self into all discourses. This means that whenever we look at an image we are at some level inserting a sense of our self through the Imaginary. Second, the Symbolic (the space where such discourses of the image are produced and are shown) is both crucial, and yet antithetical, to meaning and understanding.

This is a vital part of Lacanian psychoanalysis and we would do well to work through it more carefully, teasing out the parts that are of particular concern to us here. The metaphor of the mirror should prove to be an appropriate tool for this. For example, there is a different, although related, sense of mirroring of the act of spectating which takes place in Bernini's sculpture. For surrounding the niche piece in the Cornaro Chapel (Santa Maria della Vittoria)[c] Bernini locates members of the Cornaro family as if they are in theatre boxes, watching St Teresa. This visual frame, where onlookers, surrounding the image, are presented within the image, is a common device in the Baroque.[9] What gives the Baroque image particular relevance here is its chiaroscuro effect so perfected by Caravaggio. For here is a device that symbolically shows the liminal status of the spectator both within and outside of the image. In Caravaggio's works the in-between space of light and dark is not necessarily one of sinister ambiguity, where those in the shadow are seen as possible threats or of moral and ethical inexactitude. For part of the revolution of Caravaggio's style is the turning of the liminality of light and dark into complexity and depth.

There is something very Lacanian about such a use; psychoanalysis, via Freud, notes that ambiguity dominates our sense of the unconscious. This is the same subjective state that the three prisoners must operate within during the puzzling out of the discs. They are neither imprisoned nor free, in the dark or light, but have the possibility of both depending on their capacity to solve the problem. In a similar way the films of David Lynch, David Cronenberg, and even Hitchcock, work on positioning characters and events in a zone that is neither light nor dark. It is the emergence of shadows into the normalcy of the world; *Blue Velvet* (Lynch 1986), *Existenz* (Cronenberg 1999) and *North by Northwest* (Hitchcock 1959) show the chiaroscuro effect of horror as it positions the unknowing protagonist in a world of sex and death. Each of the main characters in these film examples is located initially in the world of 'more normal than the normal'. Their lives are defined precisely through this lack of excitement. They are then placed in a threatening position which reveals that the security of their world order is a fragile and illusory thing. What swirls them into this other world of shadow is death and/or sex. This takes us to another significant point regarding the Baroque and Lacan, that of *jouissance*.

St Teresa and the gangsters

When Lacan uses *The Ecstasy of St Teresa* to illustrate his point about *jouissance* he is working towards one of his most complex positions in terms of ethics, morality, and the conflict between the social order and our own desires. Midway through the 1959–60 seminar (putting it 25 years prior to the same sorts of analysis in *Encore*), entitled *The Ethics of Psychoanalysis*, Lacan engages in the issue of how we live in a social order that requires us to constantly keep check on our unconscious desires. It is part of the demands of psychoanalytic theory that starts with Freud's *Civilization and Its Discontents*, and is figured here by Lacan as how such a theory and practice can contribute to an understanding of ethics. In this sense it is a very specific analysis (the ethics of psychoanalysis) as well as a far-reaching one (how can psychoanalysis help us to understand the development and function of ethics and ethical behaviour). To this end Lacan speaks of the *jouissance* of transgression – that is, of the pleasures and pains involved in transgressing the Law (capitalized to designate the Symbolic's ordering of morality). As Lacan puts it so succinctly:

> We are familiar with the jouissance of transgression, then. But what does it consist of? Does it go without saying that to trample sacred laws under foot, laws that may be directly challenged by the subject's conscience, itself excites some form of jouissance? ... What is the goal jouissance seeks if it has to find support in transgression to reach it?
>
> (Lacan 1992: 195)

Extraordinary questions these, and ones that Lacan spends the remainder of his seminar dealing with. For here is the idea that excessive pleasures may well need a sense of transgression in order to operate.

Without transgression there can be no *jouissance,* and yet in all these pleasures there must be a sense of the forbidden. This is the passage from the sense of the need to do good as it conflicts with the unconscious drives of the libido and mortido (the sex and death drives respectively); it is also part of the fundamental premise of Freudian psychoanalysis – the revolt against the Father (that is, the figures of authority seen as those who create and sustain laws) in order to be able to express one's own desire. In this sense it is the transgressive force of the Oedipal act, which at the same time becomes one of conforming to the socialized sexual identity. This is the crucial part for psychoanalysis – the compulsion to conform to the Law, which simultaneously demands an exceeding of it – through desire, through conflict, through the very substance of subjectivity.

This strikes us as a very Baroque approach, for it is the tensions of conformity and excess that drive the spirit of this artistic movement. The Baroque sentiment of St Teresa in Bernini's sculpture captures this transgressive aspect, which is why Lacan (some 22 years later in *Seminar XX: Encore*) uses it to explain the difficulties of knowing about *jouissance* whilst at the same time experiencing it. As he puts it:

> ... it's like for Saint Teresa – you need to go to Rome and see the statue by Bernini to immediately understand that she's coming. There's no doubt about it. What is she getting off on? It is clear that the essential testimony of the mystics consists in saying that they experience it, but know nothing about it.
>
> (Lacan 1998: 76)

Here we find, preserved in the stone face of a saint, the unconscious – that which we all experience but can never really know or perhaps even understand.

The contradiction – the dangerous and compelling contradiction – is that *jouissance* is necessary for us to exist as desiring subjects and yet impossible for us to obtain as socialized subjects. It can only ever be seen in a mediated, sublimated version, for *jouissance* itself represents an ultimately destructive experience. It is part of the plague that Freud and Jung spoke of under the shadow of the Statue of Liberty.[10] Bernini's sculpture of St Teresa plays this out because, from this Lacanian perspective, this woman's exquisite pleasures exist as a challenge to social norms and (religious/metaphysical) beliefs. They are part of the represented contradiction between pleasure and transgression.

This may seem a long way from the point of mirrors, but in fact we have never really left the issue of reflexivity. Consider the opening scenes of *The Godfather* (Coppola 1972) and *Miller's Crossing* (Coen Brothers 1990), the latter a sort of parody/homage to the former. The characters address an unseen or obscured character (so rendering it in effect an address to the camera, especially in the case of *Miller's Crossing*) in a Caravaggioesque chiaroscuro lit room – dark with ambiguous sources of light. The topic of their address is nothing less than the moral and ethical behaviour of gangsters, and in particular the transgression of the Law of the criminal underworld. It is a device that is carried on in the television series *The Sopranos*, although interestingly it takes the form of Tony's psychoanalysis.

This direct (and, for a while, monological) address by the gangsters shows so many of the themes we have been dealing with: there is the mirroring effect of the spectator as the image looks back to us; there is the ambiguity of the image as it sits in half-darkness; there is the ambiguity of ethics and transgression; there is the signification of power and powerlessness, of entreating the more powerful to act; and there is the imminent pleasure of the transgressions (the forthcoming narratives of the films as well as those for the gangsters themselves). What is mirrored in such scenes is not simply the act of looking at the image (and it looking back at us as spectators) but the whole issue of the *jouissance* of transgression. Such transgressions are always best shown within the chiaroscuro of the Baroque because the threats involved are always tempered by the excessive delights and pleasures promised. Mirrored in such images is our desire and compulsion to transgress, and, as has been intimated here, this cannot take place in a domain of either/or (that is, of binary oppositions of good/evil, right/wrong, pleasure/unpleasure and so on) but of gradual twists into and out of the dark and light. Such twists and turns render the whole discourse beyond the Law, beyond the moments of signification that tie it to the Symbolic – or at least attempt to wrest themselves from it. This is a most Lacanian of themes, and one that we also witness in the Baroque.

This significant feature of Baroque work is the spiral effect. This is the drawing of the gaze upward (obviously heavenward) in a resistance to the high Renaissance system of hierarchy and order. For the Baroque swirls and folds, and resists the sense of conforming lines and structure. The famous mathematical dimensions and 'rules' of Renaissance art (such as the symmetrical divisions and repetitions within the painting) give way to curves and lines that fold in on themselves; they resist the Law of the hierarchy and produce an almost chaotic sensation. Perhaps this is part of the reason why it created such a sense of unease in the spectator (particularly when it first appeared) for it devised a trajectory for the gaze that took it in directions not usually devised. These swirls and folds are more than an excess of ornamentation however. They are a representation of the sensibility of the Baroque form, for they contain within them a philosophical notion.

In many Baroque designs (especially in domes as the figures fly towards heaven as well as look down on the gaze of the spectator) this involved a *trompe l'oeil* effect, which became particularly prevalent in Dutch painting of the Baroque.[d] The famous still life paintings rely on the *trompe l'oeil* effects as they arrest time (all the excessive food and flowers on display with no sense of decay) and appear to jut out from the canvas. Cloth, food and utensils fall over the edge of the table on which they are seated, certainly a showy effect to demonstrate the skill of the artist, but can also be seen as part of the spiral effect – this time coming towards the spectator. Similarly the play of light as it reflects from metal (jugs, plates, and so on) is a device not merely to add a dimension of realism but to push the elements of the painting back into the world. This light reflected on a plate is one that supposedly shines behind the shoulder of the spectator, and so becomes a shared source of illumination.

In many of these constructions we find the spectator's gaze once more being confronted directly by a returning gaze, either a literal one or one operating more metaphorically (such as the reflected light on the objects in a still life). So angels and saints look down at us from the interior of the domes, the dignitaries peer directly at us in Rembrandt's paintings such as *The Syndics*.[e] The assertion of the gaze out of the image that we see in so many Baroque works has an interesting resonance with another of Lacan's ideas. This is the contesting of the gaze, of the *dompte-regard*, of the tricking of the gaze. *Dompte-regard* is Lacan's idea of the laying down of the gaze, a sort of pacifying of the spectator. Lacan argues that this is an essential feature of the image (his example is painting but it seems to hold true of a great many 'constructed' images) and its relationship to the spectator. It is a line that we shall consider further in the chapter on Foucault, although that will have a different sense of power to it. Lacan's idea of *dompte-regard* is directly tied to one of the fundamental aspects of psychoanalysis – that of desire. And we can extend this to argue that desire is one of the fundamental aspects of the image, for that is a constitutive element of any visual culture. Perhaps one of the definitional aspects, then, of visual cultures is their relationship to desire in the image and spectator. Desire in *dompte-regard* is not simply the desire represented within the painting (or image), but also the spectator's need of desire which is met by that image. At the most formal level this taming of the gaze is required so that we can make sense of an image. Narrative cinema demands a laying down of the gaze so that the spectator can 'understand' (that is, make sense of) cuts, edits and montage; perspectivism in painting relies on the spectator laying down the gaze so that the illusion of space will make sense.

Beyond such formal examples *dompte-regard* can also be seen as a fundamental part of desire within the image that is enforced on the spectator. Just as the spectator makes sense of certain visual constructions (such as depth of field in painting) by acceding to those principles, so that process also becomes part of defining subjectivity. What we find desirable, pleasurable, abject, terrifying, and so on, is part of this taming of the gaze. We become the spectator of pleasure, for example, by accepting those images that culture deems pleasurable. Our gaze has been brought into a position where it 'sees' pleasure, because that is what has been determined, and continues to be determined, in the visual culture. To find pleasure in what are deemed culturally unpleasurable images is to resist that determination of the *dompte-regard* of pleasure. In some respects this is the role that has been given to art and the aesthetic – to push the tamed gaze in directions it is not used to, or does not expect.

Narcissism and the ego

In the previous section we witnessed Lacan's story of the three prisoners, and of how they had to enter what he terms a third time period in order to solve the puzzle. There are two other time periods, each determined by a type of positioning of the subject and each in turn related to the relationship of the self to others. To illustrate this Lacan picks up his analysis of the Edgar Allen Poe short story 'The Purloined Letter' and gives it an interesting twist.[11] What we are interested in here is how this might be read in terms of mirroring the self, particularly in terms of the narcissistic field. By turning to the issue of narcissism we are in fact continuing to develop this interest in the metaphor of the mirror in psychoanalytic (that is, Freudian and Lacanian) theory. The narrative in the story refers to a schoolboy who excelled at a particular game called 'Odds or Evens'. The object of the game is to win marbles from the other contestant by guessing whether they hold an odd or even number of marbles in their hand. This boy won all the marbles in the school because he could reason, through ascertaining the intellect and personality of the other child, what would be held up next. Dupin, the hero of the story, asks the boy how he can be so sure of the intellect of the other person (which he achieves through identification with the competitor), to which the boy replies:

> When I wish to find out how wise, or how stupid, or how good, or how wicked is any one, or what are his thoughts at the moment, I fashion the expression of my face, as accurately as possible, in accordance with the expression of his, and then wait to see what thoughts or sentiments arise in my mind or heart.

(Lacan 1988b: 180)

Here we have an interesting version of the act of mirroring, and one that is not dissimilar to the Baroque effect. The boy who wins marbles mirrors the other person's expression, feeling their emotions; the ideal spectator of the Baroque also mirrors the emotional forces. And, as we observed above, this is also the common feature of the spectator of horror films, comedies and thrillers. Once more it is important to note that this is beyond a simple identification with the protagonists, and what we are seeing in such processes of the image is a type of mirroring of the self within the act of spectating and the image. This relates to Lacan's idea of the third time that the prisoners must experience in order to win their freedom.

The three time periods marked out by Lacan are: the first time period in which the other subject is in the same position as the self in thinking and feeling; the second time period in which 'a less partial subjectivity is manifested. The subject is in fact capable of making himself other . . . he has to place himself in the position of a third party, to get out of being this other who is his pure reflection' (Lacan 1988b: 180); and the third time period in which the subject becomes capable of thinking both as the self and in terms of the other subject. Lacan describes this last position as 'something like divination' (Lacan 1988b: 181); it is the time (and position) of the prisoner who realizes the solution and the boy who can win all the marbles. This third time is the extraordinary moment that allows the subject to be both self and other. Our interest here in all of this is how Lacan's description of the third time (where knowledge of the self and other subjects takes place in a moment of reflexivity) is a type of mirroring, but based on an action of the ego and narcissism.

Narcissism is one of the most perfected forms of mirroring and offers great analytic potential in this reading of the image. We need to go beyond the restricted sense of the term as self-love and consider how narcissism operates within this relationship of spectator to image. Part of this will be the third time, when the subject (as spectator) locates the elements of the image (that is the other subject) as part of the self. Or, put another way, just as the boy in Poe's short story wins the marbles by mirroring the other competitor's expression, and the prisoner wins his freedom by mirroring the position of the other prisoners, so the spectator draws all the elements of the image into a reference of the self. The image of light as it reflects on a plane of metal in a Dutch still life becomes the light shared by the spectator in order for the illusion to work. There is also something narcissistic in the ways in which cultures produce images. Many of the culturally defined images (that is, those that come to represent the culture to itself, as well as to other cultures) are sent out in order to return. What they return is the gaze, the image of the culture itself, and the idea of a cultural identity. Images such as these range from the overt, such as flags and other national identities, to the images of the everyday. An advertisement and a television programme operate narcissistically because they are primarily concerned with showing a culture to itself, and in doing so form a relationship of the subjects of that culture to themselves. In this sense narcissism here denotes the centrality of the subject for the subject in the act of spectating. Before we continue with this line let us observe a few key points from Freud, for he is responsible for devising an altogether originary idea on narcissism.

Freud moved narcissism from its position, in psychoanalytic theories, of perversion to one that is a universal and even necessary part of human sexuality (what Freud terms a primary narcissism). For Freud, narcissism is sustained into adult life and is fundamental in the development of love relations with others; in this sense all our relations are derived from the initial position of narcissism. The original paper, *Zur Einführung des Narzissmus,* (completed in 1914) was a crucial development of many of Freud's ideas.[12] One of these is the relationship between the two drives of the libido and ego. This relationship is fundamental to the idea of narcissism. It is the negotiation of the two drives that determines, in Freudian theory, the object of love, of how we love (and are loved) and the choices that are made in love.

Reading this paper on narcissism one is struck by the prominence of the self and love, and of the significance of the cultural order of the masculine and feminine. The topic of narcissism gives Freud the opportunity to investigate further the issues of love, the self and gender. It is little wonder, then, that this is the paper that pushes further the ideas on feminine sexuality as it is composed within a social context. Central to this is Freud's idea of the distinction between the anaclitic (or attachment) type of love-object and the narcissistic type (see Freud 1984: 81). The first of these is when the object of love and desire comes from an 'outside' image (Freud's examples include 'the woman who feeds him, the man who protects him' (Freud 1984: 84)); the second when it is turned towards the self. But an interesting aspect for our study of the image lies just beyond this, when Freud makes what seems to be a passing comment on women and narcissism. It is a passage worth pursuing for it has a certain resonance with the ways in which images of the beautiful (in both men and women) have been constructed in all forms of media.

Freud, in reference to beautiful women and their narcissistic qualities, states: 'The importance of this type of woman for the erotic life of mankind is to be rated very high. Such women have the greatest fascination for men, not only for aesthetic reasons, since as a rule they are the most beautiful, but also because of a combination of interesting psychological factors. For it seems very evident that another person's narcissism has a great attraction for those who have renounced part of their own narcissism and are in search of object-love' (Freud 1984: 82–3).[13] This is the sense that primary narcissism remains as a sort of desired for state, repressed and mediated in the movement towards socialized sexuality. The beautiful narcissistic woman, for Freud, becomes an image that allows the observers the opportunity to experience afresh the narcissistic drive of their own self. This is a drive that has been if not completely repressed, at least controlled and tamed.

Let us consider a few examples of this and merge them with the earlier discussion on mirrors and the Baroque sensation, for it is already apparent that we are dealing with terrain that is interconnected. Three examples, drawn from quite different sources, will help illustrate how this process operates in different contexts. Our examples will not be solely feminine, for much of what is revealed in the beautiful narcissist is also true of the masculine.[14] It is also important to recognize that we are not so much concerned with literal representations of narcissism but rather an altogether different sort of reading. Our key point is the line from Freud when he states that the appeal – the seductive nature in fact – of such images is that they allow the spectator to revisit his/her own narcissistic feelings. For our concerns here this is the seduction of the spectator not simply by the image, but through a relationship to their own self. This is the narcissistic dimension of the third time, where self and other are observed at the same moment and become the frame of reference for solving enigmas, creating relationships and interacting with the world.

The Baroque rose kiss

When Lester Burnham sees Angela for the first time in *American Beauty* (Mendes 2000), as she dances with the cheerleaders at the basketball stadium, the world vanishes, diffused and impersonal light becomes focused and accentuating, brash sound becomes corporeal (it is as if it is within his head and wafts dream-like), public display becomes private vision. In effect Lester experiences nothing less than the powerful seduction of narcissistic beauty, embodied in Angela but encased in his own sense of self. From that moment on Lester changes his world and plays out the ego-centric drives and narcissistic desires of his past. He admits that he just wants 'to look good naked', but at the same time he pursues with a passion lost time and a version of the past that allows him to possess beauty. Certainly Angela represents a version of Freud's beautiful woman who is fascinating through her narcissism (in Angela's case this is her own misrepresentation of sexual prowess, again in a slightly hysterical sense), but it is Lester who demonstrates the drive to experience the renounced narcissism. Furthermore, Freud points out that it is in the child that we witness versions of narcissism that are attractive because they seem beyond the cares of the adult world. This is how we experience Angela – neither adult nor child – and Lester's retreat back to his own childhood. This is also why Lester's character holds so much appeal to the spectator; we do not see him as irresponsible and lecherous (although there are certain scenes of discomfort that allow a questioning of the relationship between him and Angela) but we are allowed a glimpse into the pleasures of revisiting narcissism.

It is this playing out of the travails of such a revisitation that *American Beauty* deals with throughout its narrative – it is the struggle within the third time of self and other. So, for example, when Lester becomes the hamburger server (a job that resonates with connotations of the teenage lifestyle) he becomes a version of himself as well as the other subject of his own past; he also becomes a distorted version of a cultural stereotype (teenager/college student) that translates into a type of cultural narcissistic role. This is the wonderful irony in the scene where he catches his wife and her lover as they drive through to collect their food – he is the middle-aged married man discovering an illicit affair, just as he is the teenage boy looking for love and finding out he has been jilted.

Lester's narcissistic revisitations illustrate another aspect of Lacan's theories of the mirror stage, of human subjectivity and the crisis of the self. This is when narcissism, so much to do with the development of objects of love, is played out in terms of the body:

> What did I try to get across with the mirror stage? That whatever in man is loosened up, fragmented, anarchic, establishes its relation to his perceptions on a plane with a completely original tension. The image of his body is the principle of every unity he perceives in objects. Now, he only perceives the unity of this specific image from the outside, and in an anticipated manner.

35

> Because of this double relation which he has with himself, all the objects
> of his world are always structured around the wandering shadow of his
> own ego.
>
> (Lacan 1988b: 166)

We have already seen Lester's wandering shadow (his version of himself in the past, his sense of escape and freedom, his love of Angela) and how this creates a double relation with himself. We have also already seen how Angela also creates a double relation with herself (sexualized and virginal) through her body.[15] Within this narcissism we also observe Lacan's insistence on the body as the primary frame of reference.

Both Lester and Angela interpret all object relations (including other people, their own social and sexual positions, and cultural signifiers of their lives) through their bodies. One of the best examples of this is the cinematically disguised exchange between them in the kitchen. Initially what appears to be their first kiss is revealed to be a fantasy by Lester, shown when he pulls the rose petal from his mouth. This is Lester's fantasy version of his own body and through this fantasy we witness the centrality of the corporeal. This fantasized Lester, who pulls rose-filled kisses from his mouth, is the double who anticipates. And all of this takes place within a highly Baroque sentiment and representation. The contrast to the American middle-class suburbs is Lester's Baroque experiences with Angela – the vibrant red of the roses, the fecund and bountiful petals that flow from the ceiling, and the music from his fantasized erotic encounters all perform this Baroque sentiment. Compare, for example, this rose petal kiss to Caravaggio's techniques in *The Death of the Virgin*.[f] The chiaroscuro effect, the opulence and excess, the spiralling sensations of movements from reality to dream and back to reality, the sweeps of red; or of Rubens' *Rape of the Daughters of Leucippus*[g] with its symbolic use of red (the gold cloth on the ground becomes the sharp red of the soldier's cape, and so sexually powerful) and the curious sexual interplay between the masculine and feminine (we say curious because of the almost lack of a sense of rape within the image).

Let us now take up a second example, this time engaging in a more culturally driven issue. The idea of one culture's version of another is played out in a myriad of representations and forms. The European colonial versions of the Orient[16] (and of other cultures such as Australia, the Americas, and so on) is but one of many possible examples. What then of the versions a culture produces of itself? What are the narcissistic implications of self-representation? One interpretation of this would be nostalgia, for the recreation of lost times invariably includes a frame from the reproduction.

Nostalgia has a narcissistic function because it allows for a re-experiencing of the past through a specific position. And just as individuals will have those reflexive moments of nostalgia, so too will cultures. In fact this is one of the primary functions of a visual culture – to reassert the past through a particular perspective. This reordering of past times and events contributes to the cultural now by performing the narcissistic process. Historical monuments are good examples of such narcissistic cultural nostalgia because they exist not simply to remember the past, but to allow its reinvention in terms of the now.

The narcissistic erotics of celebrity

Our final example takes us somewhat full circle, for here we are focusing on the transformation of the body into the celebrity body through this field of narcissistic fascination and desire. Central to this is the idea that what makes the celebrity body different is precisely its capacity to allow the spectator to revisit his/her renounced narcissism. This is in part the ideality of that body – that is, desired because it suggests a version of the self in an idealized form, loved narcissistically – and in part the doubling of the self (once more, this notion of the third time) so it can experience self and other. In this sense we read/define *celebrity* as a version of narcissistic desire, played out in the transformation of the body not through identification but through the merging of the twin drives of the ego and libido.[17] The spectator does not simply desire the celebrity, but is attracted (perhaps even compelled) by this potential for narcissistic release.

The word celebrity, from the Latin *celeber*, means celebration and festival, as well as crowded and populous (in terms of space), and famous. So we are not far from the spectacle of the carnival. The version of the carnival as one of social inversion, of anarchy and disruption, of free-flowing pleasures as well as dark disturbance, is one well established by Bakhtin.[18] This carnivalesque tradition acts as a release to the social constraints and repressions of the social order – it is the moment when desire and disruption overtake order and containment. Socially managed celebrity may seem a long way from the sorts of carnivalesque moments as, for example, the spectacle of the scaffold, the excesses in films by Pasolini or Oshima, and even the *jouissance* of St Teresa in Bernini's statue.[19] And it is fair to say that much of the hegemonic process of the manufacture of celebrity operates precisely against such a carnivalesque reading. But this is the fundamental issue with such a social process; celebrity, in its modern form, exists as part of a long established pattern that attempts to position (and in doing so curtail) excess within the social order. The status of the modern celebrity is a hegemonic one whereby the incredible machinery of its production continually locates it back within the social order. Yet this long tradition of celebrity has an undercurrent which is far more carnivalesque. This is the dual nature of the status of celebrity – on the one hand it acts to bring into conformity those that have been designated as different, and yet it must always acknowledge the potential for disruption.

When the Marquis de Sade finally exceeded the protection of his title he was incarcerated in the asylum at Charenton, where he would write and direct plays that would be performed by the inmates. It became fashionable for the French nobility to go to the hospital to watch de Sade's plays and these moments of excess became popular not because of the quality of the play (or indeed acting) but because of the celebrity of the author. In this curious mix of hegemony and carnivalesque we witness the operation of celebrity that is not unique to de Sade, but an integral part of this status. De Sade works as

37

a good example because the tension between the dual nature of celebrity is quite apparent, but this same sort of tension can be seen in many examples. Images of Angelina Jolie,[h] combined with tales of her tattoos and the necklace with a vial containing some of Billy Bob Thornton's blood around her neck, continually reaffirm her as carnivalesque, and yet they are positioned within a discourse of celebrity that also makes them 'safe'. Fashion magazines and Jolie's Hollywood films (from *Hackers* (Softley 1995) to *Girl, Interrupted* (Mangold 1999)) produce a certain type of celebrity that holds the discourse in the same way as the walls of Charenton held de Sade.

The mirroring effect of celebrity depends on the duality of excess and curtailment because it is derived from the same psychical operations of narcissism. Both Freud and Lacan maintain throughout their works the distinction between narcissistic drives (the libidinal and the ego), to the point where Lacan actually speaks of two narcissisms.[20] The key issue of the two narcissisms is expressed by Lacan as: 'the relation between the constitution of reality and the relation with the form of the body' (Lacan 1988a: 124); this relation, Lacan goes on to say, is 'identification with the other which, under normal circumstances, enables man to locate precisely his imaginary and libidinal relation to the world in general' (Lacan 1988a: 125). (Here it is important to remember that the imaginary relation Lacan is referring to is that of the image/*imago* and not that of the imagined/fantastical.) So here we find the idea that two narcissistic relations develop, both aimed at working through and sustaining the subject's relationship to others and the world through the drives of the ego and libido.

How does this fit in with our reading of celebrity as a dualism of carnivalesque and hegemony? One of the primary functions of the mirroring process is to establish and allow the relations of self and world/reality to operate, premised, significantly, on the form of the body. When the spectator engages in the discourse of celebrity (and this will include the full range from obsessive fan to disinterested observer who can still acknowledge that there is a phenomenon of celebrity taking place) he/she is operating narcissistically. By this we do not simply mean the projected identification of the self into the glamorous (or otherwise) world of the celebrity, but the capacity to experience the renounced pleasures (which continue to be *in potentia* carnivalesque) of their own narcissism. Angelina Jolie and the Marquis de Sade allow a constitution of reality, for the spectator, through the body that is both excessive and restrained. And this can take place – that is, celebrity is formed – precisely because of these processes of the two narcissisms.

Angelina Jolie may seem to be a unique, and perhaps biased, example of this. After all as an actor and personality she continually demonstrates, and plays on, a certain discourse of excess. She is certainly not alone in the history of cinema to have this quality – from Louise Brooks, through Bardot to Beatrice Dalle in the feminine, and Rudolph Valentino, James Dean, Marlon Brando and Eminem in the masculine – there has always been a certain type which is devised around excess. However, it is important to recognize that this same sense of narcissism and cultural duality (of excess and restraint) can be seen to be operating wherever celebrity functions, and not just in the more transparent cases. The supposed purity of someone like Ingrid Bergman still holds the carnivalesque because she is positioned, via celebrity, as the beautiful woman narcissistically driven. This illustrates the fact that the image does not have to be a literal representation of narcissism (the self-reflexive and loving gaze into a mirror or pool of water) to have this quality. In the case of celebrity it is the processes of social production that fulfil the role of the mirror; that is, the spectator is required to look at these images narcissistically in order for them to have pleasure, for them to function within the social sphere, in short for them to be able to exist as images at all.

This idea of celebrity being essentially narcissistic helps to explain its function as both carnivalesque disruption and cultural restraint. The celebrity is the agent who is allowed to act beyond the Law (that is, the social organization of law, morality, ethics, senses of order and hierarchy, and so on), but only on the Imaginary plane (that is, of the image and within the idea of the self). By considering it in this way, another part of celebrity can be explained, which is the sense of the love of the image of the celebrity. There can be little doubt that this is what the social function of celebrity allows – the erotic relationship. This is what Lacan argues in terms of all erotic relations: 'We regard narcissism as the central imaginary relation of interhuman relationships. . . . It is in fact an erotic relationship – all erotic identification, all seizing of the other in an image in a relationship of erotic captivation, occurs by way of the narcissistic relation' (Lacan 1993: 92–3). This is an extraordinary twist, for Lacan takes the Freudian idea that the appeal and fascination of narcissistic images is their capacity to experience repressed forms of love and emphasizes that *all* erotic relations are derived from narcissism.[21] The status of celebrity recreates narcissism within the spectator through this process of erotic captivation.

The most overt example of this is when the body of the celebrity is seen to be a sort of *uber*-body where its components exceed those of the normalized body (that is, not simply the body which is not part of the celebrity, but the body which is positioned in contrast to the celebrity, or the condemned, or mad). In these erotic terms it is the cultural phenomenon of seeing parts of the celebrity body or how they are placed within a certain discourse. Examples of this would include the injured body parts of sports stars (David Beckham's foot injury just prior to the 2002 World Cup); nudity in films is divided into the non-celebrity body (less significant and more mundane – the cinematized 'normal' body of extras and supporting cast) and that of the exposed celebrity (Halle Berry in *Swordfish* (Sena 2001) and *Monster's Ball* (Forster 2001). This differencing of body parts works through the processes of excess (the celebrity body's nudity seems to be more naked than that of the normalized body) that, once more, can be seen as a foregrounding of the narcissistic relationship of the spectator. The point of the nudity is not that there is exposed flesh, but that the flesh itself has been transformed – it has been named (Halle Berry's breasts, Bruce Willis's penis (in *Colour of Night* (Rush 1994)) and so forms part of the spectator's relationship to the object. Lacan's assertion that all erotic relations take place in terms of the narcissistic means that eroticism itself is only possible if the spectator operates in this way. Otherwise there is no interest in the image for the spectator.

Notes

1 This seminar is particularly relevant to any study on Lacan and the visual. In the section entitled 'Of the Gaze as *Objet Petit a*' Lacan maps out his theories of subjectivity and desire in terms of the visual.

2 The period of high Baroque is more defined, lasting the 50 or so years between 1650 and 1700. The end of Baroque is usually seen as the emergence of Rococo and then into the Neo-Classicism of the eighteenth century.

3 As one art critic has put it:

> The figurative arts of the Baroque period, especially in Italy, are governed by an aesthetic that considered art as a means of expressing the passions of the soul. Psychology made considerable progress in the seventeenth century, and the problems of the passions preoccupied a number of philosophers. Biologists laid down the first principles of physiognomy, and several artists or critics formulated treatise on expression. . . . These treatise indicate how the technique of art should render the various passions – love, suffering, anger, tenderness, joy, fury, warlike ardour, irony, fear, contempt, panic . . .
>
> (Bazin 1964: 23–4)

4 See, for example, *The Interpretation of Dreams*, where Freud discusses the connections between objects and people through simultaneity in time (Freud 1986: 424). Here Freud points out how dreams employ the painting device of showing a group of people who existed in different time periods. The relevancy for us is that dreams find it necessary to construct such temporal systems.

5 For those of you who are curious about the solution, see Lacan's seminar.

6 See Chapter 5 where we speak of Barthes' idea of the text of *jouissance*.

7 See Lacan, *The Four Fundamental Concepts of Psychoanalysis*, where he recounts the story of Petit-Jean and the fishing trip. The returning gaze of the sardine can is what we find in these images that do more than return our gaze – they devise a completely new one to look at us.

8 We have written elsewhere on the Mirror Stage and the formation of the subject in terms of the gaze and the image (see Fuery 2000). The essential feature of Lacan's theory being dealt with here is that at around the age of 18 months the subject is confronted with his/her own sense of the self – either with a literal mirroring of the self or through a more metaphorical means. At this point the subject enters into the process of socialization (of desires and drives) and acquisition of language. From this point on we are trapped in an interplay between our antisocial desires and the Symbolic order of repression and curtailment. Lacan designates this part of the Mirror Stage as the Imaginary – that is, dominated by the image. There must always be a sense of reflexivity in this process of the Imaginary for the image is dominated by the sense of the self.

9 We discuss this phenomenon of the frame and its shifting status as a part of and apart from the image in the chapter on Derrida. Other examples of this in Baroque works include the whole process of positioning figures and events within frames, and then frames (of observers, spatial elements, or symbolic objects such as clouds) around them.

10 The famous, and possibly apocryphal, story is that on their first visit to the USA Freud turned to Jung as their ship passes the Statue of Liberty and said 'Don't they realize we are bringing them the plague?' It would seem that Freud was quite aware of the European-ness of psychoanalysis, and such a comment demonstrates his belief that it was never meant to be a theory of cures.

11 Lacan deals with Poe's short story in 'Seminar on "The Purloined Letter"'.

12 Around this period Freud's works become more self-reflexive, with key ideas – such as those found in the essays on sexuality – being revisited and renegotiated. In this paper we also find crucial ideas on the ego ideal, which later becomes the theory of the super-ego.

13 Related to this, elsewhere Freud speaks about how hysterical women are often the most beautiful: 'The majority of hysterical women are among the most attractive and even beautiful representatives of their sex . . .' (Freud 1984: 94). This is a sentiment played out in a great many images of hysterics in cinema – Beatrice Dalle (in *Betty Blue*, Beineix 1986), Catherine Deneuve (in *Belle de jour*, Buñuel 1967), Natassia Kinski (in *Cat People*),

Angelina Jolie (in *Girl, Interrupted*, Mangold, 1999) – it would seem all periods of cinema allow for the extraordinarily beautiful hysteric. Freud's own descriptions of Dora are themselves filled with desirous intimation of her beauty.

14 This issue of the narcissistic aspect of the feminine is far from unproblematic. Freud, in what it is fair to say is one of his few gestures of patriarchal self-reflexivity, evens offers the following: 'Perhaps it is not out of place here to give an assurance that this description of the feminine form of erotic life is not due to any tendentious desire on my part to depreciate women' (Freud 1984: 83). By aligning some of Freud's key points with representations of the masculine here we are not trying to perform some sleight of hand, or over-simplify what is a very complex psychoanalytic theory of sexuality. Our concerns are with the relationship of spectator and image, and specifically at this point in the acts of mirroring that take place in such a relationship. What we lose in terms of the sexual analysis and differentiation (of Freud) we hopefully gain in the analysis of the spectator. That said, it is important to recognize that Freud himself specifies that the points regarding narcissism are just as pertinent to the masculine.

15 It is noteworthy that this film is populated with characters that have narcissistic tendencies developed through the shadowy parts of themselves. This includes body image (the daughter, Jane), homosexuality (Colonel Fitts), negotiation of relations through a lens (Ricky), and the need to be commercially successful (Lester's wife, Carolyn). However the 'purest' version of this Freudian narcissism occurs in Lester and Angela.

16 Perhaps one of the best examples of this is Delacroix's representations of North Africa. See Edward Said's commentaries on these in *Orientalism*.

17 In terms of the cultural position of celebrity (for they invariably do have this social function) it is significant that the celebrity body often measures a type of hegemonic desire. This is not always positive, but it is usually filled with fascination.

18 See Bakhtin, especially *Rabelais and His World* where some of the historical aspects of the carnivalesque are mapped out.

19 Consider, for example, Pasolini's *Salo* (1975) and Oshima's *In The Realm of the Senses* (1976) where the body becomes something beyond the known and acceptable. These are cinematic manifestations of Foucault's ideas of the scaffold, not as an apparatus of social control, but of the body confirmed as something that needs to be controlled and contained.

20 This is an extensive discussion and one that will take us too far from our direct concerns. The reader is directed to Lacan's seminar entitled *Freud's Papers on Technique*, in particular the section 'The Two Narcissisms'. The model of the inverted bouquet, devised by Lacan here, is discussed in terms of cinema in Fuery, *New Developments in Film Theory*.

21 It is important to recognize the sense in which the term 'erotic' is used here. Lacan's distinction between *eros* and *agape* takes us some of the way, but the issue is in the ways in which the erotic is tied to the libidinal drive. The erotic, then, is part of the libidinal economy and should not be seen solely in terms of sexualized images and relations.

a Bernini, *The Ecstasy of St Teresa*
http://www.i-a-s.de/IAS/Bilder/Bernini/Teresa.htm

b Caravaggio, *The Conversion of St Paul*
http://www.kfki.hu/~arthp/html/c/caravagg/05/30conver.html

c The Cornaro Chapel (Santa Maria della Vittoria)
http://www.boglewood.com/cornaro/xteresa.html

d For general reference to *Trompe l'oeil*
http://www.nga.gov/press/2002/exhibitions/deceptions/imagelist/images.htm

e   Rembrandt, *The Syndics*
    http://www.abcgallery.com/R/rembrandt/rembrandt121.html

f   Caravaggio, *Death of the Virgin*
    http://www.kfki.hu/~arthp/html/c/caravagg/07/45death.html

g   Rubens, *Rape of the Daughters of Leucippus*
    http://www.exittoart.nl/framesetmain.htm?http://www.exittoart.nl/gallery1.htm?http://www.exittoart.nl/rubens/rubens07.htm

h   Angelina Jolie's tattoos
    http://www.geocities.com/Hollywood/Club/8261/women/a_jolie.html

Chapter Three

TRANSGRESSION, ABJECTION AND THE BODY

Kristeva and the visual

Julia Kristeva's works are complex and deeply embedded in linguistic, psychoanalytic and literary theory. What this chapter aims to do is to look at how some of Kristeva's theories have influenced and shaped the new discipline of visual cultures and contributed to a visual theory. In Kristeva's work, the development of some key concepts holds a great deal of significance for the image and we will work through these, referring to some of her early semiotic and later psychoanalytic works. As most of Kristevan theory is concerned with psychoanalysis and its application to (predominantly French) literature, there is a need to be cautious with any application to visual cultures, as primarily this was not its original focus. However, fundamentally, Kristeva's concepts are theoretically solid, some left carefully ambiguous, and they deal with the formation and developments of the subject. In this spirit we will take up some of her key concepts, notably abjection, the body and *corps propre*, the *sémiotique* and Symbolic, and apply them to the various images forming a visual culture and a subject involved with a visual culture.

It is critical to appreciate and understand Kristeva's conception and theoretical stance on art in general, in addition to situating a visual culture in terms of wider cultural spheres. One of Kristeva's main theoretical objectives is concerned with the dynamics of how a subject or subjectivity is created *as a process*. Her work deals not so much with what the subject creates in terms of culture, visual or otherwise, but how the process of subjectivity formation influences and participates in the process of culture formation. In this way, art, or for our purposes here, all images which together form a visual culture, are discussed as forming part of a process instead of presupposing a visual culture. More simply, Kristeva's focus can be directed towards how a visual culture generates particular individuals, as well as socio-cultural subjectivities, instead of visual cultures being created or established by individuals or through a cultural collective. By keeping within this framework and consciously maintaining such a perspective, we can apply Kristeva's theories and their respective influences towards a visual culture and the 'spectating' subject.

The primary concern will be to examine the analytic strategies that appear in Kristeva's texts for reading such images, while maintaining a concentration on considering visual cultures as a process regarding the formation of subjectivity. These analytic strategies deal with issues of corporeality, abjection and disruption discussed with regards to the image, both in terms of its representation and textual strategies for problematizing it.

ABJECTION

> All abjection is recognition of the want on which any being, meaning, language or desire is founded.
>
> (Kristeva 1982: 5)

What does Kristeva 'fuse' together in her theoretical works so that the theory comes to influence and bear significance for visual cultures and visual theory? In her work on abjection, it is the working through of the abjection of self that is interesting for visual cultures. Her major work that deals with abjection is *Powers of Horror*, where Kristeva aligns conceptions of abjection with the formation of the self and subsequently subjectivity, and this is what is noteworthy when thinking about a visual culture, particularly for the position and involvement of the spectator of images, and how watching or reading these images shares in a process that promotes the formation of both visual cultures and the subject.

As most of Kristeva's ideas and theories presuppose knowledge about Freudian and Lacanian theory, it is worthwhile exploring their contribution to the foundations of her work so that her perspective has direction. To a large extent, the work Kristeva delivers in *Powers of Horror* is a response to and elaboration of Freud's *Totem and Taboo,* as well as some of his other works; Lacan's theories of the subject, and in particular his ideas of the Imaginary (with the centrality of the ego), Symbolic (the cultural order), and Real (the domain of the unconscious and all its manifestations);[1] certain aspects of Hegel (which, once more, is a key part of Lacanian theory);[2] and the anthropological works of Mary Douglas. We do not need to delve into these works in order to apply Kristeva's semiotic and psychoanalytic works to theories on and regarding visual culture, although we do refer readers to the enjoyment of reading them. Generally, these texts influenced Kristeva's research and provided a significant basis for her theories on the relationship between the subject and cultural order.

It is important to contextualize these foundations of Kristeva's theory as initially some of her writings can seem confusing and hard to grasp. Kristeva's notions of the self come from, and are developed as a result of, her Freudian training. As a result, her model of self and subjectivity is premised on loss, separation and want (or desire). This is important as it forms the foundations for how Kristeva develops her theory on abjection and its extreme, horror. For Kristeva, this fusion of abjection with a Freudian sense of self[3] allows each notion to highlight and complement the other. Coupled with abjection, this Freudian self and any sense of loss, separation and desire is heightened to the point where it focuses on the formations of the subject's psychic self, which is 'revolting' for the subject. This notion of 'revolt' is central to abjection, the abject self, and the influence abjection brings to a visual culture. One of Kristeva's main research interests looks at how the 'unnameable' achieves representation, and her work on revolt involves analysing the representations that stem from a subject's unconscious where their desires and wants are given freedom of expression.[4]

Some terms

Before we move onto the 'unnameable', phobia and revolt, and their place in terms of abjection, it is useful to locate Lacan's involvement in Kristevan thought, especially in terms of the social order – namely, society and culture, their structure and laws, and what this means for the subject. Before a subject forms its identity and becomes a socialized part of the social order, they must acquire language. For Kristeva, Lacan, Freud and other psychoanalysts, the acquisition of language represents the move away from the Mother and a successful entry as a subject into the Symbolic order. The Symbolic is a Lacanian term that refers to the arena of language, where laws and orders all contribute to the production of a subject and their identity via their institutional practices that prescribe social meanings. Put more simply, the Symbolic is the social order that rules culture and attempts to control the subject and their formation of identity through the use of language, in all mediums, including visual cultures. (Although we will argue that certain visual cultures are afforded the opportunity for rebellion against and because of this Symbolic order in the third section of this chapter, where we discuss the *sémiotique*, the Symbolic and visual cultures.) Visual cultures are indebted to the Symbolic as some typologies possess the potential for a space where a subject can present representations and images whether or not they conform to the rules and regulations of the Symbolic. Indeed at their most obvious level visual cultures are played out at the level of the Symbolic.

Relative to the Symbolic order is Lacan's Imaginary. In this domain, the ego ideal is formed, or in other words, the cultural 'I'. The subject's conception and psychical idea of what their identity is and can be represented by and through, is formed here. The term Imaginary is not used to signify what is imaginable or imagined, as this is what comes under the cultural control of the Symbolic. Instead it is better to view the Imaginary and the Symbolic as orders that relate to and support each other structurally in the constitution and maintenance of the subject's identity. Third, and arguably the most complex term of Lacan's configuration, is the Real. The closest a definition can come to describing the Real is through affiliating it with the workings and function of the Freudian unconscious. In this way, the Real cannot be represented or expressed as such within the Symbolic order. The Real refers not to what we can see, touch or read, but rather what is with us all the time – the only real reality, that of our individual unconscious. Through this structure, it is the Real that exists prior to any acquisition, or intervention, of language and, consequently, the entry into the Symbolic order.

Providing a framework for these terms is highly relevant for any working of Kristevan theory, especially in investigating her influence for visual cultures, as so much of her work relies on a solid understanding of this Lacanian structure. Kristeva's development and extension of the Symbolic/Imaginary/Real triangle is the important influence for visual cultures and visual theory as her work is concentrated not so much on analysing the subject-in-search of their other (as Lacan does), but rather looks towards the incredibly complicated process of how the subject's Real (unconscious) is manifested and represented through mediums such as visual cultures in the Symbolic order.

This is a good point to move on towards the construction of abjection – Kristeva's 'unnameable', phobia and revolt – where she deals precisely with how a subject psychically deals with such an integrally problematic issue to their sense of self – how to represent or articulate that which cannot be represented or expressed.

The unnameable, phobia and revolt

The unnameable for Kristeva (put very simply) is what cannot be symbolized. However, that is too simple a definition to work with as most of its subtleties and complexities go ignored. Within its psychoanalytic context, the unnameable is the term Kristeva uses to describe the lack that castration embodies. In this regard the Mother's lack of a penis is the basis for the unnameable as her lack is unrepresentable; as John Lechte puts it, 'her difference cannot be symbolized' (Lechte 1990). The subject's inability to express or articulate the unnameable creates the phobia for the subject (specifically here, the phobia is the fear of castration) and Kristeva argues, 'From the start, fear and object are linked' (Kristeva 1982: 33). This is important for abjection as it deals with the subject's creation of their identity, their self, and also raises the issue of fear – Kristeva's term phobia – as part of this identity formation. Through identifying how the unnameable, phobia and revolt configure and interact with abjection, the formation of a subject's identity can be worked through more clearly in terms of locating it within visual cultures and visual theory.

If phobia and object are always linked, as Kristeva argues, then part of the subject's desire to express or represent the unnameable must find a symbolic form, an object, to fill this void of fear. What the subject uses as the object to represent the unnameable is attached to their fear and serves to arbitrarily represent what could not previously be represented – the phobia stemming from difference of the Mother's lack and the phobia of separation from the Mother. In this way the void of fear is 'filled'. Kristeva uses Freud's case study of Little Hans (Freud 1985) to illustrate how the subject's fear of the unnameable is given expression through the attachment of fear to object. In the case of Little Hans, his fear is attached to the object of horses. This expression of fear is located not in a verbal signification system but in a visual signification system. 'Incapable of producing metaphors by means of signs alone, he produces them in the very material of drives – and it turns out that the only rhetoric of which he is capable is that of affect, and it is projected, as often as not, by means of *images*' (Kristeva 1982: 37, original emphasis). But what is abject about this phobia and object metaphoric connection? The horses for Little Hans function as a metaphor for his fear of castration and separation – the unnameable – and Kristeva terms this location of phobia of the void into a metaphor as an 'abject-referent' (Kristeva 1982: 38). This term 'abject referent' conveys that the phobia of the unnameable is manifested through an object and this object is the abject-referent. It is abject because this metaphor is in the form of an object, and disrupts the operation of the Symbolic through continuously forming metaphors to avoid the fear of the void of the unnameable. The production of metaphors representing phobia and revolt (or fear and its repulsion) are used to keep abjection contained. This use of 'phobia as abortive metaphor of want' (Kristeva 1982: 35) highlights the subject's insecure and unstable system of signification. Their ability to represent the unnameable has as its aim to keep abjection under control, or at the very least abated, through controlling their fear through a metaphor for its expression.

If we look at how such abjection works within visual culture, we are drawn into the confines and restrictions of the Symbolic order. The only space for expression and representation exists within Symbolic space, yet visual cultures carry the potential for rebellion and revulsion against these spatial rules as they rely on more than language to convey meaning. Through images the visual form of communication still upholds laws and practices of the Symbolic, yet also relies on their fluid and unstable representative states for communication. In the American television programme *Buffy the Vampire Slayer,* we find an example of how the abject can be represented within the Symbolic.

For Kristeva, the corpse is the most abject signifier. It threatens the subject with death and shakes the stability of both individual and cultural identity within the Symbolic order. Spike, a vampire, embodies this abjection as he represents the ambiguity of the *corps propre*,[5] life and death. He is human and non-human, alive and dead, soul-less[6] and morally torn. He exists both within and outside the social order of Sunnydale (the place of middle-class American existence) and disrupts the discursive practices of good versus evil. If Spike represents and gives expression to what is corporeally abject, then it is Buffy who epitomizes the culturally abject. She judges Spike for all his abject existence, yet is absolved from peer judgement despite her sexual relationship with him. She lacks credibility in her image and identity as vampire slayer. Her persona has become a facade and as a result the 'slayer' directive of the 'do-good' gang is infected with abjection. Culturally they despise what they slay but their identity as 'good slayers' depends on and is moulded by involvement with abjection.

This sense of the abject in *Buffy* raises the issue of phobia and its connection to the abject in Kristeva's work. Here what is linked to the subjectivity of Buffy (as vampire slayer) and the corporeal and cultural abjection of her actions (sleeping with Spike) is fear. Buffy fears her abjection and connects it to Spike. What Buffy is frightened of is what she can't name. Buffy is afraid of the void of her mother, and the position she has been thrown into by her friends and Dawn (her sister). Why is this fear then manifested in Spike? Spike represents for Buffy what she feels she lacks – control, desire, power. Buffy condenses her cultural abjection and corporeal abjection into Spike as a signifier of both. Spike is inseparable from her identity as vampire slayer, his existence and connection to Buffy is a constant affirmation of what she is supposed to be – upholder of good, destroyer of evil, and morally consistent. When Buffy is with him, her identity as slayer is spoilt, threatened, and the system and order of vampire slaying is compromised in favour of her fear. In this sense Spike also becomes part of the seductive quality of abjection.

As Buffy cannot name her fear – how can she symbolize or represent a fear of the void of the Mother, and separation from it? It is through her condensation of abjection that Spike becomes an 'abject-referent' (Kristeva 1982: 38) for Buffy. Spike never becomes wholly integrated within the Symbolic order and remains as a form of abjection for Buffy and all her friends. What makes Buffy abject is not that she desires Spike (as a clear expression of such feelings would actually signify that she can name her desire and therefore retain her identity, system and order of vampire slayer intact), but that what she desires (her mother and a fulfilment of the void she feels from the separation from her) cannot be symbolized and is displaced onto Spike, who is a referent for the abjection she feels.

Revolt

Any form of metaphoric illustration or representation that would stem from a subject's unconscious is concerned with establishing an identity through this form of imagination. The desire to establish an identity and to represent the unnameable (which in this context necessarily emerges via the unconscious) threatens the Symbolic cultural and social order. Kristeva argues that such transgression is subject to codes and impositions within the Symbolic order and this revolt that the subject experiences is a reaction to the regulation of their unconscious desires and representations. 'The metaphor that is taxed with representing *want itself* (and not its consequences, such as transitional objects and their sequels, the 'a' objects of the desiring quest) is constituted under the influence of a symbolizing agency' (Kristeva 1982: 35). There is a dual implication involved with revolt however, that keeps these Symbolic regulations of the representation of unconscious expression constantly moving outwards so that the conceptions of revolt remain ambiguous. For the subject, the Symbolic as revolted *against*, through rebellion against law and order, and revolted *by* because of the imposition of such law and order and the taboo that these effect, is always changing. In many ways no other cultural process matches the speed of such accommodations of alterations than a visual culture within the socio-cultural Symbolic order. This is in part to do with the primacy of the visual to the subject.

In attempting to represent the unnameable, the subject is in a process of negotiating with their unconscious. Symbolic law and order do not control the unconscious and as such what the subject desires to represent is not representable within culture. This is abject in its delimitation of a concrete and stable identity or readable image. As Kristeva argues, what 'causes abjection [is] what disturbs identity, system and order' (Kristeva 1982: 4). Kristeva is arguing the abjection of self does more than bring horror and revolt into the consciousness of the subject but rather, 'all abjection is recognition of the want on which any being, meaning, language or desire is founded' (Kristeva 1982: 5), meaning that for the subject, abjection is crucial in determining its cultural positioning and response to itself, other subjects and other objects within that culture. For Kristeva, abjection is pre-verbal, existing prior to the intervention of the Symbolic, meaning that abjection is part of the subject's formation of identity before it enters the social order. For the subject, abjection must be seen to be socially and culturally constructed through all systems of signification, including language, desire, image – any system that uses signs to produce meaning, but at the same time, psychoanalysis would argue that each person has their own sense of abjection that is not recognized by others. Abjection can be culturally constructed so that it seems as though it is part of the natural order of things. For example, marriage between races in South Africa during an era of apartheid would be seen as culturally abject. However, this is not simply because it was against the law of that social order. British, American or Australian cultures legally allow such inter-racial marriages, and yet there is still a version of cultural abjection because it is seen as different. Consider how such situations are still seen as cultural and personal issues in cinema. An inter-racial marriage during apartheid can in this way be seen as revolt against the South African Symbolic order and revolt by it; similarly the films of Spike Lee can be seen as exploring that aspect of disruption.

The visual culture of film is a good example of this process, in part because it operates at an extremely popular level. Cinema has become effective in looking at why certain sets of social discursive practices are held up to be culturally abject over others. In Hitchcock's *Psycho* (1960), we find the combination of what is deemed as corporeally and culturally abject in Mrs Bates. What is deemed as culturally abject is not found directly within the image – what Mrs Bates looks like is kept hidden for most of the film, seeing only very briefly her shadow and imprint in the bed. Instead it is how culture positions us as spectators to interpret the image. It draws on socio-cultural values present within the Symbolic order that identify what is abject to what isn't, in order to influence a spectator's particular interpretations regarding a series of images. When we are shown the stuffed birds in Norman Bates' parlour we are conditioned to read them as abject, yet in themselves they possess no innate abject qualities. Certainly there is a cultural repository that is being drawn on (stuffed birds in a house will always have these connotative values of oddity and possible threat) and developed in this image. This is another example of how the Symbolic cultural discourse frames objects as abject in order to elicit such interpretations.

Abjection supports the Symbolic as it is integrally linked to the machinations of the construction of the Symbolic, through for example language and social order. Abjection needs these elements and limits in order to contest and also work against them. Abjection ignores culture's borders, its identities, its rules and its regulations through manipulation and ambiguity. To just ignore socio-cultural rules, however, and identities is not abject. What becomes abject through such disregard is a refusal to maintain its limits. How the law and order of the Symbolic is maintained becomes uncertain for abjection. Kristeva clearly outlines what her theory of abjection means for people in culture:

He who denies morality is not abject; there can be grandeur in amorality and even in crime that flaunts its disrespect for the law ... Abjection on the other hand, is immoral, sinister, scheming, and shady: a terror that dissembles, instead of inflaming it, a debtor who sells you up, a friend who stabs you ...

(Kristeva 1982: 4)

In this delineation of what is considered as abject by Kristeva, there is an acknowledgement of an inherent connection between what is abject and what is central to the Symbolic order. This recognizes the arbitrary positioning of abjection within culture and any subsequent interpretation.

Figure 3.1

For a visual culture, this suggests that through representing the unnameable, the image must be surrounded by the Symbolic in order for the abject to be recognized as abject. If we take the comic strip *Calvin and Hobbes* (1992) as an example and use Calvin's subjectivity as an example of the abjection of self (see Figure 3.1) we can see that Calvin's response to the muck is both recognition of the muck's position in the Symbolic order, recognition of Calvin in response to the muck and how, both combined, they should respond and function within a Western culturally defined context. What this comic strip also illustrates is how abjection underpins Calvin's sense of fascination. He is repulsed but compelled to integrate himself with what he sees as abject in order to disturb and test the boundaries and limits of his subjectivity for himself and within the Symbolic. Through his deeper involvement with the muck, Calvin affirms his subjectivity through returning to what is revolting because in this situation he can control what he deems as abject and his relationship to and with it. In this sense, Calvin revolts against the Symbolic order of cleanliness of the body (an idea that Kristeva deals with in depth, and which we shall return to later in this chapter) and law of identity, yet at the same time is revolted by the imposition of these laws and his need to rebel. In such a short collection of images, four to be exact, it is clear to see how an image as simple as a comic strip conveys the social and cultural ideologies that position and frame interpretation via constructed abjection.

In the *Calvin and Hobbes* cartoon, we find expression and representation of the malleable limits of the Symbolic and subjectivity within the Symbolic. Calvin represents not just a little Western Caucasian boy but the Symbolically defined subjectivity that exists in all Western cultures, the desire to rebel to integrate with what is ambiguous either through bodily fluids or a culturally defined abject matter. Filmically, James Dean in *Rebel Without a Cause* (Ray 1955) embodies this same desire for rebellion. Here Jim is revolted by and revolts against the abjection of the Symbolically constructed family order. This is juxtaposed nicely against the image of the abandoned and crumbling house where Jim finds relief and safety with his friends or 'other family'. The most striking single image of this is when he confronts his father, who is wearing an apron and rubber gloves and doing the washing-up. This is an affront to Jim (but why should a father washing dishes be this?) and focuses the abject.

Kristeva argues that the control which 'horror' exerts through abjection remains hidden and repressed within culture. Every act or impulse of desire that a subject experiences or acts upon invokes this sense of self that Kristeva connects with abjection and the original separation from the Mother, the loss of continuity and satisfaction are remembered (unconsciously). Abjection for the subject signals a return to and fascination with the repulsive.

THE BODY

To understand Kristeva's notion of the body, and its significance both to and within forms of visual culture, it is necessary to consider its development in terms of some of her semiotic works. We can apply her central notion of the 'process', both important to subjectivity and signification, throughout Kristeva's work, to the development and creation of varying visual cultures, and the growth of visual cultural theory.

The speaking subject in visual culture

Kristeva views the body as a sign, however in order to explain the significance of such a claim, language itself must be viewed as a signifying process. But this is getting too far ahead too quickly. Throughout Kristeva's work, how meaning and language, or more specifically, how meaning *in* language functions, has helped to establish the importance of the 'speaking subject'. As Kristeva argues, 'In my view, a critique of this "semiology of systems" and of its phenomenological foundations is possible only if it starts from a theory of meaning which must necessarily be a theory of the speaking subject' (Kristeva 1986b: 27). The speaking subject is a fundamental element that Kristeva works through in her theories on and about language with regard to signification and psychoanalysis. For her, the speaking subject is a fragmented subject, exposed to and compelled by Freudian drives (psychical energies) and regulated by social and cultural institutions. Kristeva offers the examples of the family structure and modes of production for these institutions, but such institutions are found wherever social function depends on, and operates within, a governed ordering.

Outlining the speaking subject, and its formation and importance to language, allows Kristeva to emphasize the process of signification and to move away from the static classification of semiotics as simply a sign-system:

> It is only now, and only on the basis of a theory of the speaking subject as subject of a heterogeneous process, that semiotics can show that what lies outside its metalinguisitic mode of operation – the 'remainder', the 'waste' – is what, in the process of the speaking subject, represents the moment in which it is set in action, put on trial, put to death: a heterogeneity with respect to system, operating within the practice and one which is liable, if not seen for what it is, to be reified into a transcendence.
>
> (Kristeva 1986b: 30)

In this complex sentence, Kristeva is arguing that the speaking subject emphasizes and realizes the potential multiplicity within a system of signification. For her, it is only through theorizing the speaking subject that we can see the effects (social, cultural, global, for example) of signification, in spite of its laws and its rules. Without this focus on the subject as a 'speaking subject', signification is likely to be viewed as a concrete and inflexible mode of communication instead of the inherently different, abstract and fragmented process that it is. It is important to see the rules and laws of signification as a system that is necessary to the speaking subject and communication, visual or otherwise. Without such regulation, the capacity for fragmentation and its expression via representation would be impossible.

In terming the subject a 'speaking' subject, Kristeva is calling to attention the subject's position and involvement in signification as well as their insertion into the Symbolic order. Placing significance on the 'speaking' aspect of the subject, their contribution to the formation and direction of meaning within cultural spheres, such as visual cultures, is highlighted and as a result the process of signification is also underlined. Any formation to the contribution of cultural meanings in a social sphere from the speaking subject involves aspects of reproduction and this is why a focus on the processes and effects of visual cultures is so important. Visual cultures create multiple spaces within larger cultural arenas and moments for challenge regarding current meanings and their forms of production.[7]

The body and visual culture

The body is produced through images in a variety of visual media – television, advertisements (both moving and static), cinema, comics and, most significantly, the moving bodies of everyday life that we pass by and look at daily. It is the body and all its shapes that comes to exemplify the questioning of social institutions, their values and meanings fashioned in the signifying practices that structure the Symbolic through such a diverse range of visual cultures. It is also in and through the body, as we have noted in the chapter on power and Foucault, that the Symbolic is displayed and maintained.

The body reflects the agenda of a visual culture through its fragmented state. Certain visual cultures possess the potential for non-uniformity and are not always readily understandable. Indeed these typologies of 'transgressive' visual cultures resist any commitment or acquiescence to social conformity, instead revolting against such strong Symbolic drives and laws. Transgressive visual cultures are not defined through their content or subject matter, despite that this will bear on the transgressive nature or flavour of the visual culture it/they appear(s) in. In identifying a transgressive visual culture, we are acknowledging and locating the potential and capacity for visual cultures, in general, to be transgressive for individuals, therefore, on a subjective basis. To say this 'visual culture' or these types of visual cultures are transgressive – such as pornography, love of car crash scenes, David Lynch films, Surrealist or Humorist art, comics like Manga – is to reduce what is, or what can be transgressive within visual cultures. Such singular and specific identification or location of transgressive visual cultures immediately locates them as operating within the confines and regulatory laws of the Symbolic order, under strict Symbolic control. By using the body as a signifier for what carries the possibility of endless transgression, the reduction in classification of what is transgressive regarding visual cultures is avoided, as the focus moves away from general homogenous groupings, towards uncovering the heterogeneity of transgression.

The body within such visual cultures reflects this schema as it becomes an embodiment of the multiplicity of perspectives that visual cultures generate. However, this is not to suggest that the body is simply a vessel for the effects and politics of transgressive visual cultures, or indeed even the stabilizing and sanitizing of the body by the cultural order. The body is an extremely effective example of visual culture, regardless of its adherence to the Symbolic order. This is because it allows images to reflect and perform the rebellions and revolutions against the Symbolic order and regulations of signification, but it also invites the acquisition of other positions, revolutions, and rebellions within visual culture not already present. The body-as-a-message, through images and everyday existence, is an invitation to the 'speaking' subjects of visual cultures. It reminds them of their capacity to alter and shift the socio-cultural meanings that they can produce or that they receive, and this is the confrontation that visual cultures manufacture in the Symbolic order.

To illustrate such a typology of functioning of the body, we need look no further than the much-debated image of catwalk models. Here we are presented with images and forms of the female body that confronted and resisted the Symbolic ideal of the body in general, and yet at the same time fulfilled a particular type of demand within that cultural order.[8] They were called too thin, too harsh, and were said to have reflected a distasteful side of the fashion world. Yet at the same time, they showed exactly what a certain agenda of fashion is interested in doing, which is to shock and introduce what is new and different. Fashion (and we take this term in a particular context here) is concerned with revolution, constantly seeking what is new and attempting always to change what it is to be 'new'. (At the same time fashion can also be said to be reactionary, conservatively aiming to preserve the status quo – this is precisely the tension between the images that allow it to exist within and potentially beyond the Symbolic.) These bodies, skeletal as they were said to be, did not bring about or cause the social transgressive waves of teenage anorexia, but illustrated the influence images have on cultural movement, social meaning and values. Representation of such corporeality provoked a response that was a result of resistance to 'normal' and reaffirmed representations of bodies, because in viewing them it required interpretative action. Such interpretative action is a mutiny by 'speaking' subjects through visual cultures against wider culture, and this mutiny is an act of a subject's conscious questioning of *their* position as a body and the result is the threat of potential change in what is considered as 'normal' and as 'reaffirmed', not just about social bodies but also about everything social and cultural.

As a meta-term, 'visual culture' is not simply about digesting images that are viewed, or looking at the historical importance of places and positions of images (although this is valuable in itself). Whilst concerned with representation, visual cultures are interested in its effect and causality on the larger socio-cultural sphere. The body moves across all cultural spaces and is part of both the Symbolic language, the language of visual cultures, and spaces of resistance. Much of Kristeva's theorizing of the body stems from a linguistic and semiotic perspective, which accounts for her concentration on its relation to language and to her other fields of interest such as psychoanalysis. It is from this outlook that we must also view the body in relation to the construction of a speaking subject if we are to understand how Kristeva interprets the body, its relevance and position within the Symbolic order.[9]

The Symbolic order, the speaking subject and the body

In order to conceive of a subject that possesses a consciousness both of itself and its surroundings, it is vital to think of language as a system produced by culture, orders and laws, as well as a system that is based on creativity, disruption and challenge.[10] In this manner, language can be seen to function as a process within social orders and cultural contextual conditions that are always in a shifting state. Visual cultures are not any different to other aspects of culture in this manner. Part of seeing language as a signifying process is to acknowledge its capacity for heterogeneity, but also to contextualize its function within the Symbolic order and adherence to its laws. In Kristeva's particular formation and definition of language, we still need to retain her Freudian sense of self in discussing her term the 'speaking subject'. For without this fundamental distinction, her conception of language as a signifying process loses its capacity for heterogeneity. Why this Freudian self is so important is that without it 'Any attempt at reinserting the "speaking subject," [into language] … resolves nothing as long as that subject is not posited as the place, not only of structure and its regulated transformation, but especially, of its loss, its outlay' (Kristeva 1984a: 24). Through this Kristeva is arguing for the element of activity that the speaking subject contributes to a signification process as it operates within the Symbolic order and subsequently language. The 'speaking subject' is the split subject involved in the process of the signifying practice of language, and in emphasizing this 'speaking' aspect of the subject, with particular reference to its involvement with language,

Kristeva acknowledges the difficulties of a subject being a part of language and at the same time being alienated by it.

Visual cultures are positioned in similar ways within the Symbolic order. They are contained within its structure and ruled by order and regulation but are concurrently alienated by these same orders and regulations through its capacity to constantly produce and provide images within the Symbolic order that threaten and disrupt its system, order and laws. This is why the body provides an excellent example as it exists dually as an image and as a viable physicality within the Symbolic order and within visual cultures, functioning as a signifier of disruption, challenge and revolt, or as a signifier of regulation. Neo is this signifier of disruption and revolt for the matrix, and specifically for Agent Smith, in *The Matrix* (Wachowski Bros 1999) as he represents the hidden fragmentation embedded in a seemingly homogeneous cultural space. It is through his knowledge of and existence within both social spaces of the matrix and the real world that Neo is allowed to achieve this dual existence as a signifier of revolt and of regulation. Neo is a signifier of revolt for Agent Smith, yet is the signifier of regulation of the Real World for Morpheus. He upholds the values and social meanings of the real world, even conforming to the fulfilment of his prophecy. It is interesting to note that he becomes most effective when he can see the matrix. In the agency of change resides the visual. Similarly, Nicky in *Casino* (Scorsese 1995) is the signifier of revolt, disruption and challenge to the Symbolic, as his presence is always connected with violence and cultural abrasion. He represents non-conformity both within constructed cinematic Mafia dialogue and law, as well as general cultural law through his conflict with Sam and his inability to function conservatively within socio-cultural discourse, and even within the cultural excesses attached to Las Vegas. This is supported through his corporeality – he is a short man whose stunted height represents his lack of cultural growth and adaptation. However, he also functions as a signifier of regulation in that he articulates the excess of Mafia warfare that formulaic cinematic representation has established.

Questioning the Symbolic: the deject body

Kristeva distinguishes between the body and the subject's rendering of the body in terms of the Symbolic. In order to be a speaking subject, our body has to exist within the Symbolic order and consent to its rules and regulations. The body resists this – and this is what Kristeva terms as the 'deject'. 'The one by whom the abject exists is thus a *deject* who places (himself), *separates* (himself), situates (himself), and therefore *strays* instead of getting his bearings, desiring, belonging, or refusing' (Kristeva 1982: 8 [*sic*]).

Kristeva's 'deject' or 'stray' is 'an exile who asks, where?' (Kristeva 1982: 8) from concurrently inside and outside the Symbolic order. 'Deject' signifies and represents the position of the subject who allows abjection to exist and invade their social order. One way in which the 'deject' questions their place in the Symbolic is through the body. Another perspective is that, as a 'deject', the positioning of the body within the Symbolic order is questioned. Within visual cultures, the speaking subject is called on to participate in the production as well as the sustaining of the body as it appears within the Symbolic order. At the core of abjection lies the abjection of self, and Kristeva sees this abjection connected to an investment in an 'ideal body' that she terms the *corps propre* (we deal with this in greater depth later in the chapter). The 'deject' reads the *corps propre* not as a separate representation of corporeality but, instead, interprets him/herself through it. 'Instead of sounding himself as to his "being," he does so concerning his place: "*Where* am I?" instead of "*Who* am I?" For the space that engrosses the deject, the excluded is never *one*, nor homogeneous, not totalizable, but essentially divisible, foldable, and catastrophic' (Kristeva 1982: 8). Any comparison with the *corps propre* will always result in an abject body, as the abject body is the by-product produced by the images of the *corps propre* that can only exist through visual cultures.

In *Manon des Sources* (Berri 1986), Ugolin functions as a deject. His love for Manon causes his separation, his situation, his place within the film's Symbolic order to be questioned. Ugolin is always asking 'Where is he?' in terms of his love for Manon. In the scene where Ugolin sews a pink hair ribbon of Manon's into his skin, we are situated in his place, forced to ask 'Where is he?' For Ugolin, his gifts to Manon reflect the deject's constant rebuilding, restructuring of his Symbolic order. He continuously seeks to define his love for Manon and his existence through it. Ugolin's love for Manon becomes a spatial comment within the film. It consumes Ugolin from the space of the village (the normative order and discourse of the film) and from his uncle, and ultimately from any form of what is considered as a normal expression or representation of social and cultural space. This results in his acts of love, such as sewing a hair ribbon into his skin, of the dead bird, to be interpreted as catastrophic acts. Ugolin, like the deject, is aware of the abject present in his shows of love, yet this awareness only compels him to try again, to offer Manon another gift of his love.

Rambo in *First Blood* (Kotcheff 1982) presents us with the body as a deject that questions the Symbolic order. Here is a body, masculine and primed for excellent physical performance in war, yet treated as a marginal body within culture. The visual force of Rambo's body creates disruption in the spectator's interpretation. Where do we locate this body? Rambo is a soldier and his body is a pure product and defining representation of what physical movement is in warfare, yet he is treated like a madman. This example is interesting as it takes the *corps propre* and reverses the sense of abjection regarding corporeality so that the spectating subject is faced with Rambo's seemingly perfect body as social and cultural dejection. (This is a body whose definition of perfection is specifically located within a precise cultural and historical moment.) Rambo's corporeality, as *corps propre*, exemplifies how Kristeva's deject reads his/her entire subjectivity through the existence of the 'perfect body'. Rambo is ready for war, Rambo *is* war because of his body.

Corps propre: bodies and abject bodies

The term *corps propre* can be translated as 'one's own clean and proper body' (Kristeva 1982: viii) combining both the connotations of what *belongs* to one's self as well as what is culturally considered clean. Through adhering to this polysemic definition of *corps propre*, Kristeva quickly establishes a sense of corporeality that exists nowhere except in cultural ideology manifested via various images and representations. Due to the inclusion of 'cleanliness' in describing the body, Kristeva keeps the *corps propre* as a representation that belongs only within the Symbolic. An interesting example of the *corps propre* is to be found in Cameron's *Terminator 2: Judgment Day* (1991).

In this film there are multiple corporeal representations, which is evidence in itself that the body is a slippery representation within the Symbolic and highlights its capacity within visual culture to disrupt the Symbolic. This diversity, heterogeneity even, resists the categorizing that is a feature of many systems within the Symbolic; consider how much language is based on systems of classification in order to communicate and generate meanings. This diversity of form is also fecund ground for abjection as it helps corporeality intertwine with corporeal identity in visual culture. The negativity of the *corps propre* is articulated through the T-1000. Its composition is 'liquid metal' and needs to function in the Symbolic order, so assumes the human form. In doing so, the form it assumes represents the bodily ideal of the Symbolic order, the *corps propre*.

The body of the policeman that is inhabited by the T-1000 for much of the film, represents the Symbolic order's laws, its borders and its regulations through its masculinity, its uniform, its clean hairstyle, its white, untanned skin, its shiny black shoes and its lack of bodily fluids. Here the signifiers of 'order' and 'law' within Western Symbolic discourse function as synecdoches for the containment, cleanliness and regulation of the *corps propre*. This representation of the body takes cultural institutions that are supposed to protect us from what is usually seen as abject and turns them into abject. The T-1000's lack of bodily fluid loss – it does not bleed from injury or weep with pus – is a good example of this. Its corporeality is completely intact, suggesting that its identity is completely intact and subject to the same contained condition. Its unity and stability within the Symbolic is never compromised, despite multiple attempts at explosion, freezing, shattering and dismemberment. It is beautiful in its form, reversing what is traditionally seen as culturally and corporeally abject. This renders all other corporeal representations within *Terminator 2* as abject. The T-800 (Arnold Schwarzenegger) can bleed, lose skin and hair, and participates in this reversal of abjection.

Whereas blood, death and decaying flesh are abject outside the filmic discourse of *Terminator 2*, within it, these images that emphasize the border of the body confirm what is not abject. Similarly, traditional characterizations of policemen and motherhood both within and outside of filmic discourse are challenged through the portrayal of their form via the T-1000. In assuming these cultural identities, what is culturally safe is challenged and subsequently read as unsafe and abject. Sarah Connor is initially framed as culturally abject by being confined to a psychiatric ward, but is redeemed through becoming a good mother to John.

For Kristeva, these constant representations and expressions of bodily fluids as transgressive (returning to our previous discussion of what constitutes a transgressive

57

visual culture) of the *corps propre* (one's own clean and proper body) are the only means through which the subject can establish their identity successfully within the Symbolic order. These abject images of the body underline the tenuous hold that the Symbolic has over expressions and articulations of the body via images, and additionally, how it constantly seeks to stabilize and organize such destabilizing fluids. Kristeva clearly associates the abject with the body. 'Contrary to what enters the mouth and nourishes, what goes out of the body, out of its pores and openings, points to the infinitudes of the body proper and gives rise to abjection' (Kristeva 1982: 108). The body is one of the primary sources of abjection, as even though the Symbolic constantly attempts to contain it, censor it and purify it, all bodily fluids negate such attempts through crossing the boundaries, borders and limits of the corporeal body. This stretching of the body's representations via fluids defies any Symbolic law and order imposed. Part of the function of visual cultures, particularly transgressive visual cultures, is their capacity to aid this subversion of the Symbolic through making any representation of bodily fluids so fascinating that such images are not simply representing natural parts or aspects of the body, but are also representing a revolt against the Symbolic. The fluid movements of the T-1000 as it moves between places, and the blood that appears on the outer layer of the T-800 are fascinating for the spectator because of and through abjection.

The unclean

One of the functions that visual cultures provide for in the wider cultural spaces is the capacity for images to articulate the abjection and horror of the individual and the Symbolic. They generate space for the abject to be expressed, articulated and represented. The advantage the image has here is that it can operate from beyond the Symbolic. When abjection, corporeally or culturally, is introduced as an image it is not always part of the abjection that forms or contests the Symbolic order. It can be an aspect of visual culture. The representation of abjection via the body, bodily fluids or other ambiguous means is articulated or represented through a non-verbal form. Visual cultures use images that are seen as culturally, socially and bodily abject as representations that are trying to bypass the rules and regulations of the Symbolic order and language, so that abjection is 'named', becomes 'nameable', through the visual medium. Turning towards a psychoanalytic frame, 'Excrement is also on the side of the "maternal" to the extent that it is the pre-symbolic basis of one's own/clean body (*corps propre*)' (Lechte 1990: 163). Waste helps to establish or suggest the body's limits but is connected to the Mother through the subject's place prior to their entry into the Symbolic order.

The body is close to Kristeva's interests as it is never far from her concerns about the Mother. The abjection of the body, via filth, waste, uncleanliness, epitomizes the separation from the Mother, highlights her existence as a non-object of desire, and provides the intervention of the Symbolic. Bodily fluids such as blood, semen, vomit and sweat all signal the corporeal boundaries and test the Symbolic and its limits, keeping both the social order and abjection ambiguous in terms of where they begin, end and meet. 'As a mother is a threat to boundaries – standing as she does for their effacement – rituals, in reinforcing identities, at the same time reinforce separation: that is the existence of subject and object' (Lechte 1990: 163).

THE *SÉMIOTIQUE*, THE SYMBOLIC, AND VISUAL CULTURES

Another way through which the body resists the Symbolic is via the *sémiotique*.[11] To contextualize the importance of the *sémiotique* to Kristeva's oeuvre, it is necessary to outline the position of abjection with regards to subjectivity. Such contextualization is significant as it helps to connect all of Kristeva's theories regarding the Symbolic, the *sémiotique* and abjection, through focusing on the significance for the subject. Before we flesh out the relativity and influence the *sémiotique* has for visual cultures and the Symbolic, it is worthwhile briefly sketching out its position in the work of Kristeva, as it is a highly complex issue.

The *sémiotique* forms part of the signifying process, its counterpart being the Symbolic. While it is seductive to seek concise definitions to unusual terms, such as the *sémiotique*, it must be resisted here. Kristeva develops this term, '*sémiotique*', to identify and extend the formation of subjectivity (as a process) and the on-going relationship the subject has with the Symbolic. Tied up with the subject-in-process are notions of drives and their energies (stemming from the unconscious), *jouissance* and ultimately death. Part of analysing the subject-in-process is a working-through of the difference between the *sémiotique* and the Symbolic.

For Kristeva, abjection is never totally separate from the body but lingers on the border of subjectivity, implying a constant threat of instability and loss of life. In this way, the Symbolic order is always threatened and always seeks to control both subjectivity and the abject. This is important for all types of visual cultures, as part of this threat is a fundamental component of the construction and expression of images. Abjection generates the possibility of expression for sublimation (a transformation of repressed material into another form such as art and music). The driving out of abjection must occur prior to entry into the Symbolic, yet it can never be fully forced out. As an obligatory part of subjectivity, abjection remains repressed or needed to be excluded from the subject if they are to function 'normally' within the normative socio-cultural discourse of the Symbolic.

The *sémiotique* not only disrupts and jars systems of language but also offers discourse space to multiply and, in turn, multiple sites of readership. It is because of the *sémiotique* that discursive practices come to form discourses, and these discourses, which form other discursive practices as part of the anarchic nature of the *sémiotique*, express its ability to create space outside of the Symbolic. This is not to posit the *sémiotique* as a reversing process but to highlight its function of operating beyond and outside the surface(s) of language and particular discourses. The Symbolic needs the *sémiotique* so that it can order, rule and contain. In a similar co-dependent fashion, the *sémiotique* needs the regulation of the Symbolic so that it can possess a destabilizing creativity not found within the Symbolic. Part of the lure of the *sémiotique* is that it seems to possess this wonderful sense of creativity and uncompromised articulation to language, as well as an underlying danger seeking to unhinge language and the subject's involvement with it. This sense of the two orders is dangerous in its simplification, although it does draw attention to the polarity within systems that the *sémiotique* seeks to challenge and disrupt. What we need to take away here, especially in the case of visual cultures, is the *sémiotique* potential for new space. A little later in this section we will come to the concept of the *sémiotique chora* that deals with this sense of space.

This distinction between the *sémiotique* and the Symbolic is highly significant for visual cultures as without the Symbolic order, and all its laws and restrictions that help to control and form identities and cultural consciousness, sustainable visual cultures would not eventuate. Visual cultures need the control of the Symbolic order so that they are able to operate within it, by using images (as a form of communication) that are produced as a series of discursive practices that form comprehensible discourse. The Symbolic cannot function alone, however, and needs the 'texture', the unrepresentable aspect of the *sémiotique*, to form its socio-cultural fabric. In these terms, we can recognize that the social and cultural orders produced by the Symbolic are also shaped by the energies and drives of the *sémiotique*.

This aspect of the *sémiotique* helps to identify the space in visual cultures for revolution. Whether it is manifested through a set of images which test, rebel against and disrupt the borders of the Symbolic, or which work towards establishing a different order, the *sémiotique* serves to maintain the potential transgression and evolution of visual culture through adapting to the constant changes within culture itself. The *sémiotique* affords the room for new forms of expression not only within clearly demarcated cultural discourses, such as literature, but also carries the potential for the cultural form of expression to change. In the 1970s there was punk, Warhol and disco – a few examples of movements that the combination of the Symbolic and the *sémiotique*, as a signifying practice, helped to identify as cultural movements and cultural expressions through the visual medium. Here we can see the *sémiotique* working to establish and maintain certain visual cultures that were culturally deemed as transgressive, yet ironically, in order to maintain their transgressive nature in the 1970s, the *sémiotique* now, around thirty years later, has to work alongside the regulation of the Symbolic to allow these images and cultures to appear non-transgressive. This feature of the *sémiotique* highlights its opposition to the rigidity of signification, instead locating its machinations with the drive for meaning rather than any enforcement of it.

Relating Kristeva's *sémiotique* to visual cultures relies on a connection based on its disruptive and anarchic qualities. One approach is to consider what it is about visual cultures that reflect this sense of the *sémiotique*, or alternatively, what visual cultures already in circulation are *sémiotique* in nature? This last aspect is to analyse certain examples from all forms of visual cultures individually, carefully working through large amounts of subject matter. To take up this task at present would detract from the one at hand, that being to investigate the notion of resistance the *sémiotique* brings to visual cultures through creativity, disruption and challenge. To answer these sorts of issues and questions, we can turn to Kristeva's work on the *chora*, where she argues the drive energies and challenges of the *sémiotique* originate from.

Kristeva's *chora*: strange space

Kristeva uses the term *chora*, found in Plato's *Timeus*, and places her own agenda on it to emphasize or draw attention to the place-ness and containment of the *sémiotique* that cannot be represented.

> Let us enter, for a moment, into that Freudian aporia called primal
> repression. Curious primacy, where what is repressed cannot really be held
> down, and where what represses always already borrows its strength and
> authority from what is apparently very secondary: language. Let us
> therefore not speak of primacy but of the instability of the symbolic function
> in its most significant aspect – the prohibition placed on the maternal body
> (as a defense against autoeroticism and incest taboo). Here drives hold sway
> and constitute a strange space that I shall name, after Plato (Timeus,
> 48–53), a chora, a receptacle.
>
> (Kristeva 1982: 13–14)

Here, Kristeva is outlining her intended use for this specific Platonic term '*chora*'. The appropriated Kristevan *chora* is a container for the drives and energies of the unconscious (hence her reference to Freud and the link to repression), which is the conflicting make-up of the *sémiotique*, and is essentially what makes the Symbolic and its existence unstable.

This is a highly complex term that Kristeva chose to attach to the *sémiotique*, yet what we can derive from it for our purposes regarding visual cultures and visual culture theory, is that in terms of the *sémiotique*, whatever is represented, articulated or expressed appears in the Symbolic. As a result, all forms of representation (whether or not they form part of the *sémiotique* processes) are products of the order and regulation of the Symbolic. John Lechte provides a clear explanation of the *chora*: 'The *chora* is a semiotic, non-geometrical space where drive activity is "primarily" located … . In particular the *chora* is the locus of the drive activity underlying the semiotic' (Lechte 1990: 129). The *chora* can thus be seen to contain, if unable to represent, the promise of revolution in terms of space. As the *chora* contains that which is repressed and denied, its expression within the Symbolic is complex, as Kristeva herself acknowledges 'although the *chora* can be designated and regulated, it can never be definitively posited' (Kristeva 1984b: 26). At the same time, however, it is important to do so if the activity of the *sémiotique* and its contribution to the signifying process is to be given any weight. Kristeva's configuration of the *sémiotique chora* is invested in circumventing the 'naturalness' of signification and seeks to undermine the stability of the space of communication and signification with the Symbolic order.

Why this configuration of the *chora* is interesting in terms of space within visual cultures is that it is still dependent on an ordering, but a paradoxical ordering. 'Though deprived of unity, identity or deity, the *chora* is nevertheless subject to a regulating process [*réglementation*], which is different from that of symbolic law but nevertheless effectuates discontinuities by temporarily articulating them and then starting over, again and again' (Kristeva 1984b: 26). The ordering of the *sémiotique chora* is regulated through what destabilizes the Symbolic – a series of repetitive disruptions and challenges (or as Kristeva argues, discontinuities). Subsequently, any engagement with this destabilizing ordering produces fragmentation in a number of ways. First, in the sites of spectatorship relating to an image, the relationships of these sites within the meta-discourse of visual cultures, and the continuous series of repetitive disruptions and discontinuities present between a subject and an image (found in the dynamics of the Symbolic and *sémiotique*).

Taking this to a concrete example, we can look at any visual medium that uses self-reflexivity in its processes of communication and signification. In the films of Woody Allen the spectator often encounters such self-reflexive moments. In *Annie Hall* (Allen 1977), for example, Allen uses an address to the camera while waiting in line for a film to reassert the comedy in his scene. By drawing attention to the code of film-making, and consequently its apparatus (both technical and socio-cultural), Allen destabilizes the site of comedic spectatorship whilst concurrently reconfigurating potential films of comedy and their future sites of spectatorship. Allen has 'effectuated [a] discontinuity by temporarily articulating [it] which in turn starts over, again and again'. Most of Allen's films at some stage function in this way, if not overtly such as stopping people in the street in *Annie Hall*, but through a similar sub-text of thinking out loud. This particular discourse of comedy operates through acknowledging Allen's dependable discontinuous style as a Symbolic order within the meta-genre of comedy. This is the form and function of the *sémiotique chora* – to deconstruct previous orderings of comedy by challenging its traditional 'order/s' only to replace it with a new order and so on. Picasso's late series of self-reflexive painting also illustrates this operation of the *sémiotique chora*.

Indeed reflexivity (particularly in comedy) is one of the 'safest' manifestations of the disruptive processes because it has this including effect. When we encounter the same order of disruption in different ways (such as transgressive violence or sexuality) it can have an alienating effect. The spectator must then choose (if such a choice is made an option) to either resist altogether or negotiate in order to gain this sense of inclusion. These resistances can take the form of censorship, repression, denial; the negotiations can take the form of reappraisal (of moral values or aesthetic judgements), strategies for inclusion (such as the commodification and hegemonic control of the new material). All of this takes place at both the level of the individual spectator and the cultural order.

Notes

1 These three terms are complex and invested in a great deal of Lacan's work. We have defined them in more detail in this book, and it is important to note that these few lines are quite insufficient as definitions. They will, however, serve as a guide here.

2 Lacan studied Hegel early in his career, and there are various moments in his seminars where this is most apparent. Kristeva shows similar roots in these ideas. This is not to suggest that either of them are Hegelian – but it is important to acknowledge this presence.

3 It is very relevant to include Freud's case study of *Fort/da* at this at point, as this is where the self and senses of loss and separation originate. To look at its relevance to Kristeva's ideas on the subject, it is worthwhile to quickly cite Lacan's mirror phase, which is a psychoanalytic theory that marks the entry of the subject into the Symbolic order or, primitively, the subject's learning of language. Very briefly, what Lacan's concise, but incredibly complex, theory argues is that around the period of 6 to 18 months of age, a child's world of fulfilment and completeness is shattered through the invasion of the Symbolic order (crudely defined as rules, regulations, order and laws of culture, society and language). Lacan's term for this is the Name-of-the-Father. This interference results in separation and loss from the child's previous peaceful and fulfilled state. Why this is relevant and important to remember when Kristeva talks about self is that for the child this separation and loss is connected to the mother. Prior to the invasion of the Symbolic, the feeling of fulfilment and complete happiness *was* the mother for the child. After this experience of loss, the child now has language and desire that will keep him/her returning to this experience forever, searching for fulfilment of desire and a sense of completeness.

4 Some of these terms, such as 'unnameable' appear obscure, especially as we are looking at Kristeva's work to see how it has influenced the development of visual theory and visual culture. While it is important to take note of these terms and locate their importance to the development and progression in Kristevan theory, what is more important is to see how the combination of the terms carries significance to a visual culture. That said, as the chapter progresses, the meaning and use of these complex terms in this way will become clear.

5 We deal more with the *corps propre* later in the chapter.

6 In later series of *Buffy*, Spike does receive his soul back but this does not detract from the point regarding abjection.

7 It is worth clarifying that the term *speaking subject* denotes a capacity regarding a subject's interaction with any system of signification, and it is for this reason that we include and maintain the term 'speaking' here.

8 It is worth noting that whilst much of the contention over the appearance of 'too-thin' catwalk models was aimed at the female body, such cultural debate raises the general attitude towards the body overall. It is also interesting that the body, when exemplifying forms of resistance, is usually manifested through the female form, signifying the cultural attitude of femininity and bodily representation of the times. Acknowledging this does not negate or make redundant any contesting forms of the masculine body, but simply draws attention to the particular example cited. Examples of the masculine form follow later in the chapter.

9 From a different angle, Kristeva deals with this in a more visual example in her essay 'Giotto's Joy'. The reader is referred to this text as it complements much of what is being discussed here.

10 The third section of this chapter – 'The *sémiotique*, the Symbolic, and visual cultures is', deals with this structural relationship in greater depth.

11 Kristeva's term, '*le sémiotique*' has been widely translated and referred to as the semiotic. We choose to keep the original French term as it helps to preserve the distinction between the wider field of semiotics and more complex and diverse *sémiotique* as part of the signifying process. As Roudiez points out in his introduction to *Revolution in Poetic Language* (1984), Kristeva demarcates between *la sémiotique* as the specific domain of semiotics as the general science of signs – containing the other aspect of the signifying process of language – the Symbolic, and its antithesis, *le sémiotique*.

For all films refer to
http://www.imdb.com

Chapter Four

FROM PARASITOLOGY ☐
TO SPECTRES

Derrida and the visual

LOCATING DERRIDA

As we have expressed elsewhere, part of the concern of this book is to consider the relationship between culture and the visual, of how cultures are produced through the visual, and the ways in which we can utilize visual signs to read and interpret cultural processes. So the term 'visual cultures', to reiterate, does not simply refer to the visual texts of a culture, but rather a complex system that at some level must involve examining what it is to engage in such interpretative acts. Included in this is the idea that we need to examine the visual products of a culture in order to understand cultural processes, including the formation of the spectator. Thus, our use of the term 'visual cultures' (combined with the interests of critical theory) always carries with it a reflexive sense about meaning and understanding. As discussed in the chapter on power and Foucault, an image never simply is, but involves a relationship between image, context and spectator. At some level the image invests, exerts, struggles with, and operates within a sense of power, which necessarily includes the struggles with interpretation. The central concern in this chapter is how certain versions of critical theory can be employed to try to map out the relationship of the image to understanding and interpretation – two processes very much immersed in processes of power. We will also be interested in how one of the major figures of contemporary philosophy – Jacques Derrida – has used the visual in his systematic teasing apart of the major issues of philosophical methods. This, then, is the inversion: we look to see how the image can be used to explore issues of philosophy, and how philosophy has used the image to work through its themes. The central figure in all of this is Derrida.

One caveat before we go any further. There have been many philosophers concerned with all aspects of the visual, and the obvious question is 'Why consider Derrida above any of the others?' Some of the reasons have already been outlined in the introduction to this book – that is, the locating of a particular moment (that is, the various movements in critical theory) in terms of the visual, and the defining issues of culture. But it is also noteworthy that what Derrida offers is a way of looking at the large-scale themes and histories of ideas. If his ideas – perhaps erroneously (or at least ambiguously) termed deconstruction[1] – can be said to have a recurring theme it would be one of how systems of thought and methods of analysis need to be examined from the inside out in order to understand how they attempt to produce meaning. Part of this deconstructionalist technique is to expose the rule governing processes of a system of thought. So, for example, to see how a certain philosophical (indeed any) line of thinking develops a way to seem more true, more valid and validated, than other systems. This will be the issue at hand for this chapter – how we might explore deconstruction's relationship to the visual; and included in this is a consideration of the ways in which deconstruction might be used to explore the image. A key part to all this will be the idea of seeing how Derrida's systems and techniques of analysis can be used to explore the image from the inside out, and of how images gain a certain status (such as the true image, the sacred image, and so on).

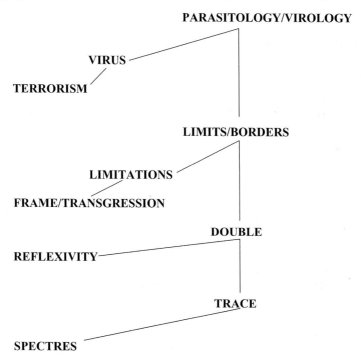

One of the most seductive – and dangerous – strategies of bringing someone like Derrida to a study of visual cultures is to take up some of the dominating terms and work them into a study of the image. So, for example, Derrida's term of *différance*[2] might be used to explore differences and deferrals in the image. However, the problem with such an approach is that it runs the risk of eliding the real sense of what is going on in Derrida's work. It is rarely a good idea to lift such complex terms from their context and attempt to utilize them in a manner for which they were never really intended. That said, there are extraordinary insights to be had if one can work the terms through the texts, in our case that of the visual. With this in mind our proposal here is to attempt to capture some of the flavour of Derridean deconstruction by taking up some recurring themes and applying them to issues of the image. The diagram above represents how we might progress through this, moving through four interconnected themes: parasitology and virology, limits and borders, the double, and the trace. The diagram in one sense moves 'downwards', from the broadest sense of deconstruction as a parasitology, through to a very specific issue within deconstructionalist texts – that of the trace. The diagram also moves 'sideways' towards connected terms and ideas before we encounter some possible examples. These include the metaphor of the virus and rupture as deconstructionalist techniques/processes; and from these the two examples of terrorism and symptom. At the next level we find issues about limitations and boundaries, exemplified this time through the frame and transgression. The third level deals with the double, with the examples of reflexivity and the uncanny, which in turn are connected to the final level of the trace with its sense of spectres.

Parasitology/virology

Derrida once responded to an interviewer's question (regarding his work and communication) with the following:

> I often tell myself, and I must have written it down somewhere – I am sure I wrote it somewhere – that all I have done, to summarize it very reductively, is dominated by the thought of a virus, what could be called a parasitology, a virology, the virus being many things. . . . The virus is in part a parasite that destroys, that introduces disorder into communication. Even from a biological standpoint this is what happens with a virus; it derails a mechanism of the communicational type, its coding and decoding. On the other hand, it is something that is neither living nor nonliving; the virus is not a microbe. And if you follow these two threads, that of a parasite which disrupts destination from the communicative point of view – disrupting writing, inscription, and the coding and decoding of inscription – and which on the other hand is neither alive nor dead, you have the matrix of all that I have done since I began writing.

> (Derrida 1993: 3)

In this beautifully succinct passage Derrida indicates the two aspects that typify *all* of his work – the disruptive and the liminal status, expressed in these terms as that of neither living nor dead.

It is easy to see why Derrida's works can be taken to be inherently destructive or negative when he admits that of primary interest is this issue of the disruptive. However, it is important to recognize that deconstruction – or any of the aspects of Derrida's themes and techniques – is not about the destruction of ideas and systems, but a genuine attempt to come to terms with them. It is significant to remember, for example, that the term deconstruction has its origins in Heidegger's *Destruktion* and Hegel's *Aufhebung*. Both these terms carry within them not a negative sense of destruction, but of rebuilding, of growth and change, of shifting orders. Hegel's *Aufhebung*, for example, has three 'meanings' to it:

to negate, to preserve, and to uplift. Thus it is never simply a matter of destroying the ideas, but exploring their trajectory, their methods and processes, and how they function. (We shall take up this term in more detail later in this chapter.) The original meaning, and intent, for all these terms is not to destroy but to alter. Take, for example, this passage from *Of Grammatology*:

> The movements of deconstruction do not destroy structures from the outside. They are not possible and effective, nor can they take accurate aim, except by inhabiting those structures. Inhabiting them in a certain way, because one always inhabits, and all the more when one does not suspect it. Operating necessarily from the inside, borrowing all the strategic and economic resources of subversion from the old structure . . .

> (Derrida 1976: 24)

For Derrida, it would seem, the most effective way of understanding and altering a system of thought is to be within it, rather than external to it. This is a strategy that is very well known in many guises, and we shall return to it through some examples in a moment.

So why does Derrida choose the negative-sounding analogy of the virus for his work? Recall that the first quality Derrida specifies for his virology/parasitology is that it 'introduces disorder into communication', and that it disrupts destination.[3] This sort of enterprise is most markedly demonstrated in works such as *The Post Card: From Socrates to Freud and Beyond* (hereafter *The Post Card*), where we witness, through an extended analysis of the love letter and psychoanalysis (especially Lacan and Freud), the idea of the disruption of communication and meaning. One of the key aspects of this that Derrida develops in *The Post Card* is the *lettre en souffrance* (the lost letter, or one held in abeyance). Derrida's theme is one of the letter that does not, and cannot, arrive at its destination. This is not a failure of a particular type of letter, but the idea that no letter – no sign – ever arrives at its intended destination because of the disruptions to the communication process; or, perhaps more accurately, every sign has the potential to become a sort of *lettre en souffrance* through this technique of deconstruction.[4] Part of Derrida's technique is to expose and work through this sense of non-arrival for all systems of meaning and interpretation. This is how it is phrased by Derrida in the particular instance of the letter:

> The mishap of this perhaps, is that in order to be able not to arrive, there must be included in the idea a force and structure, a drift in the destination, such that it must also not arrive at all. Even by arriving . . . the letter carries the sense of not arriving. It arrives elsewhere, always, several times. You simply cannot take hold of it. That is the structure of the letter.

> (Derrida 1987a: 135)

So even when we seem to have a hold of the letter – that is, in effect, to have understood and gained meaning from something – for Derrida it will always contain within it a certain non-arrival, a certain multiplicity of arrivals in other places. Elsewhere Derrida states: 'a letter does not always arrive at its destination, and from the moment that this possibility belongs to its structure one can say that it never truly arrives, that when it does arrive its capacity not to arrive torments it with an internal drifting' (Derrida 1987a: 489). Let us now take up this idea of the torment of internal drifting in terms of the visual.

The torment of internal drifting: terrorism

After September 11, and the Bush administration's declared 'war on terror', images of two very different orders were constructed, but both were directed at a very specific target, with deliberate intentions. The first of these were the images of the terrorists themselves, the second of various Western leaders and public figures with Islamic people and cultural artifacts. This was the intended destination of these images/letters – a war on terror, not the West against Islam. The internal drifting of the two sets of images is contained precisely within their juxtapositioning in the world's media, and the torment was precisely the danger of not linking the two in the intended manner. It was important for this letter's arrival (the winning over of the public mind and sympathies) that the images of the terrorists be seen as evil, but not as external. The force of the 'war on terror' lay in the internalizing of the fear that acts of terrorism could continue to take place. Significantly this fear was generated in a great many Western countries as if it was something new; whereas the truth is that many of these countries (such as Britain, France, Italy, Spain, Germany) have had a long history of terrorist activities within them. However, running parallel to this was the idea that internalized Islamic culture (in the USA, in Britain, etc.) is good. This was further mirrored by the highly simplifying notion of good Afghanistan people against the bad Taliban regime. Any slippage from reading the images in this way – that is, the internal drifting – would lead to an ambiguity of meaning. This has the effect of a sort of terrorist *en souffrance* – held up and yet to arrive, as well as the cause of suffering. This is the sense in which all terrorist acts operate, in this constant state of arriving.

We are not directly concerned with the actual politics of the images, and, as much as one can, we cautiously put to one side the difficulties of the histories and ethics of such a situation, in order to stay focused on the idea of reading images of terrorism in terms of non-arrival. For both terrorists and those who fight them are caught up in the same struggle of the image. As Umberto Eco once pointed out, the difference between the criminal (such as the bank robber) and the terrorist is that the latter needs to be recognized and seeks the exposure of the media, whereas the bank robber will always try and keep his/her identity a secret. This is why terrorist groups and those who oppose them (almost inevitably governments) compete for control of the image, fearing and acknowledging the internal drifting of arrival and non-arrival. Terrorism is a particularly good example of the vying for interpretative power in the image, as well as revealing just how much the image conveys beyond the words that surround it. After September 11 (even the date has now become a self-standing sign) the image of the fundamentalist terrorist was so emphatically entrenched in the world media that it could evoke very specific responses. Yet competing with this are the two forces of the internal drifting – the need to construct an image of non-terrorizing Islam for the West, and the need to assert the absolute sense of danger in the terrorist.

We witness a remarkably similar process in the terrorist's construction of the image, including how much slippage is involved in the manifestation and interpretation of those images. The targets on September 11 were chosen as much as images by the terrorists than for any other single reason, more perhaps than as politically or strategically damaging. The Twin Towers were already established images, existing in so many of the visual representations of New York (and synecdochically, the USA), and the terrorists would have known that their acts would be captured in a variety of media. And it is the images of those towers that remain most vivid in people's minds. This construction of the image is how the terrorist attempts to control the internal drifting of the message, and the world's media, by replaying and reproducing those images, attempts to reconfigure them in a directly oppositional way. The difficulty of course – and this is an 'of course' added by deconstruction – is that this internal drifting is not only a fundamental part of any act of communication, it is also essential. Deconstruction does not create such internal driftings, such moments of indecision and complication in the sign, but it does work to expose them and to acknowledge their existence.

This example brings us to a difficult point on deconstruction's capacity to analyse (the image or any other form of the sign), for it leads us to ask the question as to how one is supposed to perform such a deconstruction. To understand precisely what is involved in this difficulty it is important to distinguish between two models of analysis. The first is perhaps the version that most of us are used to – that is, a system of tools is brought to bear on the problem or issue and through them we make sense and produce interpretation. But strictly speaking it is not really possible to perform such a process with deconstruction. For deconstruction is not really about taking up a text (be it an image or a document, an utterance or a cultural process) and applying various processes of analysis, rather it is the *transformation* of that text through deconstruction. In this sense the whole series of images that emerge from the September 11 terrorist attack are deconstructions of the original images of two buildings in the New York skyline. The images of the Twin Towers are transformed into a rupture of terrorism and counter-terrorism, the West and Islam, and so on. In this we witness how deconstruction is the product of a new image out of the old, a rending of the seemingly seamless so that it becomes an altogether different version of itself.

At the limit

The second attribute of deconstruction's methods and systems we wish to consider is how they are always positioned at the limit. Derrida once described his discourse in the following manner:

> I try to keep myself at the limit of philosophical discourse. I say limit and not death, for I do not at all believe in what today is so easily called the death of philosophy (nor, moreover, in the simple death of whatever – the book, man, or god, especially since, as we all know, what is dead wields a very specific power).

(Derrida 1987b: 6)

So the limit is vitally important for Derrida; it does more than simply designate the extremity or the end point – it is the very marker that allows deconstruction to exist. Part of the project for deconstruction is precisely to find the limit of a discourse, and for us this means finding the limit of the image, and how the image can help us find other limits. Let us take these separately, even if in reality they are usually closely linked.

Determining the limit of the image is complex, in part because what actually constitutes an image varies enormously. The cinematic and the painterly are constituted of images, but to assert a sense of limitation for either of these would look quite different. However, there are a number of aspects that we can approach not quite in the spirit of universals, but at least within the sense of deconstructing the image. The following are suggestions and the list is far from complete – but it will at least give a sense of things. The limit of the image can be seen as including: diachronics, synchronics, exhaustion, and problematizing. Our strategy here will be to indicate how these are reflected in Derrida's works, and how we might use them in the analysis of the image. It is important to bear in mind that what all of these elements represent is the image in crisis, of how it is positioned in such a way, of how it functions, through a challenge to itself and the context from which it emerges.

DIACHRONICS

This is the study of developments across time, of evolving and shaping, and how we might compare one stage of change to another. In a diachronic analysis we are looking to the relationships established over time, as they make sense through time. A simple analogy would be a sports match, such as any code of football. If we were to watch the game as it progressed, the relationships we observe would be seen diachronically. It is beyond the direct concerns here to examine deconstruction's complex analysis of time, and how time is such a fundamental aspect of deconstruction, but a single point may help reveal something about the idea of the image at the limits in terms of time.[5]

The permutations of a diachronic analysis of an image are not difficult to imagine. Some examples might include the tracing of a representation of a certain theme or figure as it evolves across styles of painting. Compare, for example, the images of the Venus[a] from Botticelli to Velázquez's *Rokeby Venus*[b] through to recent versions such as Uma Thurman[c] in *The Adventures of Baron von Munchhausen* (Gilliam 1988) and we witness vastly different images and sensibilities. Even as the figure of Venus alters in the representations across time, it retains certain defining aspects. In this way it accumulates meanings, making some more concrete than others. Another diachronic analysis would be the impact of television on cinema. As television sets became more widespread in the home, cinema attendances plummeted. Part of the survival strategy by the Hollywood studios was to make bigger, more grand films filling up larger screens. So, for example, we can see the introduction of Cinemascope in 1953 (with Twentieth Century Fox studio's version of the biblical epic *The Robe* (Koster 1953)) as part of the historical shifts that take place which have a direct impact on the cinematic text. Here we witness an economic challenge being met through a technical invention that had an effect on the style and shape of films. We can note a similar process taking place when the VCR became popular; cinema's response was technically lavish computerized special effects. Or, as a final example, we might look at the emergence of certain fashions (such as punk) and their influence on modes of dress. A strict diachronic analysis is not such much concerned with the diffuse and heterogeneous borrowings of punk style, but more how it emerges at a particular time (in a particular culture) and how it then becomes hegemonically controlled and contained.

Our interest here is to see how deconstruction looks towards the limits of the image through this process of diachronics. In other words, how deconstruction allows us to see the diachronic shifts as a positioning of a limit. In this sense diachronic image shifts (that is, those moments in time that come to stand for a transition of one image for another) are an intricate part of defining the limit of the image, and how the emerging image deconstructs its predecessors. It is important to note that not all temporal shifts and developments do this, but what we are most interested in is how deconstruction can be used to analyse when such temporal shifts, and crises, take place. Of course part of this is to recognize that the shifts themselves are moments of deconstruction. We also need to bear in mind that such shifts cannot simply be seen as a clear-cut change from one order to another, for often there is overlap and blurring.[6] An example of this is Picasso's *Les Demoiselles d'Avignon*.[d] Painted in 1905 it has come to be seen as one of the key images in the formation of not only Cubist art, but of Modernism itself. In a way Picasso's painting only makes sense if it is read diachronically. It is positioned as a stage in the development of European art that is typified by self-reflexivity, challenges to realism, and a looking to cultures other than the European (in this case African). Its force, and this is also the force of Cubism, is gained from the diachronic positioning of limits. In this way Picasso's painting is a deconstruction of certain traditions and processes in Western art precisely because it works at the limits.

SYNCHRONICS

If a diachronic approach is the study of relationships across time, then a synchronic one is the study of relationships at one particular moment in time. To pick up the analogy mentioned above, a synchronic analysis would be the freezing of the football game at one particular moment and we would look to see the relationship of the players at that moment. In a way the slow-motion replay is a synchronic derived deconstruction within the diachronics of the overall game. Within that moment time is frozen (even in a live telecast there is a sense that nothing, of significance anyway, is taking place within the game itself), slowed and replayed. Multiple camera angles are used to deconstruct the space as well as time, so each time we revisit the passage of play, it is the same moment of time presented from a different perspective. It does seem rather overstating the case to call the slow-motion replay in a sporting event a synchronic deconstruction, and yet it is undeniable that something is happening to our sense of time when these 'sub-texts' are presented. There is this compulsion to analyse when we witness the slow motion – we are being told that this is a moment of significance and worthy of closer, slower examination. The telecast itself takes such interruptions and rather than losing the sense of the immediacy of the images actually strengthens that sense.

These two examples – Picasso's *Les Demoiselles d'Avignon* and the use of the replay in a live telecast of a sporting event – take us back to something that has been at the heart of this discussion of Derrida. We are always dealing with a double agenda when we engage with deconstruction. The first of these is how deconstruction can be employed in the analysis of images; the second is how images can be used to perform a deconstructionalist analysis. These are, of course, not mutually exclusive and often the texts will perform a sort of combination of the two. In Derrida's works we see examples of both these. A few examples of these include: *The Truth in Painting* which uses Van Gogh's image of the peasant shoes[e] to work through various philosophical issues (including key aspects of Heidegger); *Memoirs of the Blind* which covers a vast array of paintings and sketches to examine the idea of subjectivity and selfhood; *The Post Card* with its recurring analysis of the postcard of Socrates and Plato; and *Droit de regards* which explores the ideas of gender and sexual identity through a photo-montage. Positioning diachronic and synchronic aspects as formations of the limit illustrates how deconstruction can be used to examine how specific images alter the larger order of image generation and perception.

EXHAUSTION

One of the criticisms that seems to be a recurring part of deconstruction's existence and operation is that it runs the risk of pushing its analysis to the extreme, thus producing nonsense. Derrida's style is wonderfully slippery and bewilderingly convoluted, especially at those moments where he pursues the limits of a concept or idea, and it is sometimes not difficult to see how this can become resistance in itself. It is important to remember that much of Derrida's work is about language and its limitations – his is a very literary enterprise. So when he is engaging in an idea, surrounding the discussion is the sense that everything is being mediated through and in language. Derrida's strategy is to work with, rather than against, this sense of problems and limitations and include them in the process of deconstruction. As with so much of Derrida it is important to remind ourselves that his primary interest is pushing to exhaustion a concept, term, or, for us, the image, not to make it seem like nonsense, but to test its limitations and possibilities. This necessarily includes the limitations of interpretation and the possibilities beyond the known. In this we witness a key aspect of Derrida's works – the challenge to systems of meaning as they exist to produce some sense of truth. So often this allows his work a sense of opposition – which he seems to conjure out of a proposition the exact opposite of what we might be expecting.

One of the effects of such a strategy is this sense of exhausting the text. Let us try the idea, once more, of seeing how deconstruction can exhaust the image, and how an image can be seen as a type of deconstructive exhaustion. In both senses the general idea is that things are pushed to their limit, in order to find some sense of the limit. This raises an immediate problem, for how are we supposed to define a limit? What constitutes the limit of an image? Such questions are precisely what deconstruction wants us to engage with. It is not really important that a concrete, universal limit is found – in fact nothing could be further from the case for deconstruction – rather the issue is the action of investigating such limits. Deconstruction would argue that it is the function of the text to explore the idea of limits, even if such limits are impossibilities in themselves. This is much along the lines of Derrida's ideas on the centre and the margin. In *Of Grammatology* Derrida argues that the centre is ultimately just another margin for another (falsely perceived and constructed) centre.[7] So we can say here that any limit is really just another centre which has its own limits elsewhere. We will commence with some examples of an image that seems to exhaust to the edge of visual limits.

Exhausting the visual by/through an image quickly reveals itself to be an impossibility, mainly because what is being contested is not so much the materiality of the image, but our capacity as spectators to keep up with the commitment of exhaustion. When the French New Wave film-makers, and the primary case is Godard, devised the jump-cut – that jarring, disruptive edit that draws attention to the cut itself – there was a sense that he had exhausted the image produced through classical editing, including the idea that cuts between and within shots should be seamless and invisible. However, the limit that Godard tests and then exhausts in *A Bout de Souffle* (1959) relatively quickly became accepted within the cinematic process. The limit of classical editing, deconstructed through the jump-cut, was altered in order to contain this new version. In a way this interplay between institution (in this case cinema) and innovation is part of textual evolution, and it could be argued that all versions of textual development involve some sense of deconstruction through exhaustion. Another example of this are the British artists Damien Hirst[f] and Tracey Emin,[g] and the American photographer Robert Mapplethorpe,[h] who produce images that test the limits of what constitutes the artistic image. In the cases of the work of Hirst and Emin the exhaustion is the tradition of art as a representational mode by using subject matter that seems 'unaesthetic' (such as the bed and dead animals). With Mapplethorpe it is similar, because of the challenge to what is seen as suitable subject matter in art, and different because of the medium (photography) he worked in.

Apart from these formal aspects of taking exhaustion to the limit there are many other possibilities. The ethical subject matter provides an almost immediate declaration of limits (as we have noted with Mapplethorpe). To cross such a limit is to enter into what the social

73

order deems as the unethical or the immoral. In 2002 the film *Baise Moi* (Coralie (I) and Virginie Despentes 2000) became internationally famous for its explicit representation of sex and violence. Yet none of these types of images in the film are in themselves especially extreme. Somewhat ironic, the rape scene in the film (which does convey a very sordid sense of sexual violence, and is quite extreme) was hardly cited in the voices of protest over its screenings. What seemed to give the images in the film this quality was that they were being screened in mainstream, public cinemas, and the film itself became a focus of protest (both for and against its screening). The limit here was not so much the image but what images could be shown in public spaces. This suggests that the sense of exhausting the limit exists not necessarily entirely within the image (what it shows, how it is shown, and so on) but on a number of different facets. The same sorts of protests have a long history in the visual arts; Mapplethorpe's photographs, films such as Pasoloni's *Salo* (1975), Scorsese's *Last Temptation of Christ* and Cronenberg's *Crash* (1997), and the erotically charged drawings and paintings of Surrealism and Dadaism, are a few examples that show how sexuality almost always moves the image towards a limit of some sort. Even when there has not been public protest, we can find many examples of images that press the limit of the image within its contemporary context. Titian's *Danae*,[i] for example, is erotically driven and sexually explicit. The fact that it is by an entrenched artist and handles the material in a symbolic manner preserves its sense of 'art', but there can be little doubt that what is being represented is male ejaculation and sexual acquiescence by the naked woman. This is a version of the 'money-shot' in pornographic films, perhaps even the 'golden shower'!

What is significant is that so much of this process takes place in the relationships 'outside' of the image, including that of the spectator and the image, and the culture and the image. For just as images, through this matrix of the visual culture, formulate systems of representation, they also create the spaces for the contesting of such representations. How a culture defines its visual limits is as significant as the actual images it produces. The most immediate example of this is censorship, which is why something like a sexually explicit image can appear to be empty and exhausted. In one sense it exceeds the limit (of social acceptability), and yet it is also immediately exhausted because it has nothing more to show. Censorship works very much as a declared process of absence, but it is also important to remember that much that is absent is also often invisible. It is much harder to think of what a social order does not allow or contain because we are so used to the sense of a plenitude of images. However, the yet to be formed images can also be seen as part of the definition of a visual culture because they form part of the limits to an image, and because they exist in *potentia*. This idea of the absent being as important, and often more important, than the presences is a sentiment that holds true in a great deal of Derrida's work.[8]

These few short examples demonstrate images testing the limits of tradition, form and ethics. They are very restricted in their representation and only indicative of the sorts of issues that are involved. In order to flesh them out a little more we can compare these examples to what Derrida does to an image. He is concerned with using the image to progress the deconstruction of an idea, so it is not that far removed from the above examples. The text we are concerned with – *Memoirs of the Blind* (1990) – is too large for us to take up here, so we will take up a typical method of deconstruction and focus on a single moment in the book. It is a key moment, it should be noted, and in many ways one that sums up the primary issues of Derrida's concerns in *Memoirs of the Blind* as well as his ideas on the deconstruction of the visual.

Derrida, around a third of the way into the book, gives the background to the project (he had been invited to organize an exhibition at the Louvre) and how he had been seeking a theme for some time.[9] This theme he calls a paradox of the 'two great 'logics' of the invisible at the origin of drawing' which he then goes on to term the transcendental and the sacrificial:

> The first would be the invisible condition of the possibility of drawing, drawing itself, the drawing of drawing. It would never be thematic. It could not be posited or taken as the representable object of a drawing. The second, then, the sacrificial event, that which comes to or meets the eyes, the narrative, spectacle, or representation of the blind, would, in becoming the theme of the first, reflect, so to speak, this impossibility. It would represent this unrepresentable.
>
> (Derrida 1993: 41)

The transcendental, in this sense, is all of the impossibilities of representation, and all of its potential. It is the impossible because it is the *idea* of representation rather than something that has been represented.[10] If the transcendental is the impossibility of representing something (and Derrida's logic here is that representation always involves a removal from that which is being shown) – and thus the condition of attempting to represent – then the sacrificial is the attempt to represent. We sacrifice the transcendental (all possibilities) in order to represent.

To take a simple example (and perhaps one that distorts the sophistication of Derrida's argument) if we want to represent a tulip we may well commence with a transcendental sense of the flower, but we quickly sacrifice all those possibilities in order to produce the final image of that red tulip with its green stem sitting in a terracotta pot. Imagine now the full sense that Derrida is working within as he constructs these terms. The representation of love or hatred, passion or ennui – these are complex states and emotions that never lend themselves to easy representation. And each time a representation is made there is a certain type of sacrifice to the thing itself. It is important to note that Derrida is not aiming for some sort of essential understanding or expression of a thing or state of feeling – in fact this is the opposite of the case. Derrida's (perhaps somewhat ironic) example is blindness and the complexity of representing this transcendental moment (the invisibility and absence of the gaze) within different contexts (such as castration, revenge, resentment, and so on). For Derrida the theme of blindness works this idea of the sacrificial particularly well, for in blindness there is the inherent difficulty of representation. (Although it is also interesting to note that later Derrida aligns the sacrificial blindness with insight (see especially pp. 109–10 in *Memoirs of the Blind*.))

Returning to our overall theme of exhaustion, it is possible to see how Derrida, by employing these terms, explores the limitations of representation. He is not really concerned with the struggles of representation in painting, but of how representational systems overall force us to engage in a number of paradoxes involving what something is and what we actually see, of the possibilities of representing something and the sacrifices that meet our eye/gaze. In this way any attempt to represent something – every image in effect – is an exhaustion of the possible. This is not simply because the image fixes the representation, but also because ways of representing, and looking, become determined and predetermined. This is why Derrida describes the event, that is the moment, between the transcendental and the sacrificial as that which 'provides drawing with its thematic objects or spectacles, its figures and heroes, its *pictures* or *depictions of the blind*' (Derrida 1993: 41). In a sense this is the compromise of representation, as it works its way through the impossibilities of the transcendental and the demands of the sacrificial. It is also the space and mechanism which allows a visual culture. Without these two it would not only be impossible to represent, but also impossible to understand the representational processes or even what is being represented. Both the transcendental and the sacrificial become the defining paradoxes of the limits to representation.

On the double

There are many varieties and versions of the double in Derrida's works. In fact it recurs with such regularity that it quite possible to argue that it is one of the fundamentals of deconstruction. In order to understand why this is the case we shall first consider what Derrida seems to be evoking when he deals with the double, and then look to how deconstruction's theorizing of the double can be used to analyse another feature of visual culture. As with the previous sections in this chapter we will be looking towards more than the obvious examples in Derrida's works, and in doing so attempt to extend the idea of the double across a range of material. One more point before we proceed. Deconstruction emerges from philosophy; it is, in Derrida's words, an attempt to tease apart the philosophemes that have come to stand for truth, veracity, meaning, and so on. As such it must engage in the fundamentals of philosophy, including its historical arguments and processes. One of the recurring aspects of this in Derrida is Hegel, and in particular the Hegelian dialectic. Essentially this is the structure of thesis/antithesis/synthesis, or an argument or historical condition (thesis) produces its opposite (antithesis), there is struggle and from this emerges a new proposition/order (synthesis). From this position emerges a new idea (a fresh thesis) and the process starts up again. This is the *Aufhebung*, which has three connotations – to negate, to preserve and to uplift. Hegel delights in this triple meaning, and sees the dialectic as performing all of these actions. Derrida wants to deconstruct this idea of the dialectic (see especially his essay 'From Restricted to General

Economy: A Hegelianism Without Reserve' in *Writing and Difference*) and push the idea beyond the structure of binary opposites. It is this project that drives much of the argument about doubles in Derrida.

One of the fundamental aspects that we need to understand in this context of the double is that for Derrida it is rarely, if ever, a case of simply the double (or doubling) of something. There are many reasons for this, but at its core we see a fundamental theme that runs throughout Derrida's works, and one that can be traced back to the earliest (phenomenological) writings. If one of the primary aims of deconstruction is to reveal and dismantle the primary terms of reference in a particular epoch then it must do so with a reflexive eye. It is one thing to devise a strategy to reveal sense-making and rule-governing processes, but it is another thing to not see your own system falling into that same status/trap. In other words, deconstruction's attempt to expose the rules of meaning-generating systems could place itself precisely in that same position – of generating a different set of 'rules' about how meaning is generated. To safeguard against this, deconstruction must have a healthy level of self-reflection – it must observe itself as it attempts any form of analysis. Incidentally, this is precisely why so many of the writings of deconstruction seem so convoluted; it observes itself as a philosophical system attempting to disentangle all the issues of philosophy.

In this way deconstruction cannot be the double of the current systems of meaning, it must exist somewhere else. In these terms it is interesting to see how Derrida positions *différance* – a key term of deconstruction – within a group of thinkers that includes Nietzsche, Saussure, Freud, Levinas and Heidegger (see, for example, Derrida 1973: 130). Our epoch (which includes this list), Derrida points out, is one of *différance*. All of these theorists share this attribute of critical self-awareness, of a misgiving for their contemporary order's ways of thinking, and a desire to reformulate them beyond a straightforward alternative. *Différance*, we recall, is to differ and defer; it is to see that every sense of meaning operates on a process of differences, and that all resolutions of meaning should be, and necessarily are, deferred. Thus meaning itself becomes a dynamic process where production overtakes resolution as the primary force. In this way we see how *différance* is not Derrida's double of a theory of meaning, but another term altogether.

Différance is one example of many of Derrida's resistance to binary oppositions (the fundamental structure of Western thought that gives us the divisions of good and evil, male and female, day and night, and so on). Derrida (along with that broad group of theorists named as post-structuralists) provided strategies to think outside of the binarisms, including what he called the third term:[11]

> the pharmakon is neither remedy nor poison, neither good nor evil, neither
> the inside nor the outside, neither speech nor writing; the supplement is
> neither a plus nor a minus, neither an outside nor a complement of an
> inside, neither accident nor essence, etc.; the hymen is neither confusion nor

distinction, neither identity nor difference, neither consummation nor virginity, neither veil nor unveiling, neither the inside nor the outside, etc.; the gram is neither a signifier nor a signified, neither a sign nor a thing, neither a presence nor an absence, neither a position nor a negation, etc.; spacing is neither space nor time; the incision is neither the incised integrity of a beginning, or of a simple cutting into, nor simple secondarity . . . .

(Derrida 1987b: 43)

Here we have a list that reveals much more than a set of terms. Notice how Derrida ends many of the listings with an 'etc.' – even in his examples there is a sense of so much more than can be contained in the terms. One gets the impression that no matter how long the list of terms became (of the neither/nors) there must always be a sense of a furthering. Notice also how the list given by Derrida starts with some relatively straightforward binarisms (remedy/poison, inside/outside) but quickly collapses into more complex relationships that might not appear as opposites ending with 'incised integrity of a beginning/secondarity'. Derrida does this to demonstrate not only the instability of the binary oppositions, but also the difficulty of even working in terms of the binary. Finally, notice how this list of terms (pharmakon, supplement, hymen, gram, etc.) works across divisions of opposition so that what Derrida achieves is a sense of deconstruction beyond the terms and into the ways in which meaning is constructed.

This is the case where we find Derrida's engagement with these terms: for example, the pharmakon in *Dissemination*; the supplement in *Of Grammatology*, the hymen in *Spurs: Nietzsche's Style* all carry with them this sense of not just containing their own opposites, but of acting as moments of deconstruction. It will take us too far afield to pursue this much further, but just as a final point of illustration it is important to realize that in Derrida's list are embedded references and illusions to more and more ideas and arguments. Take, for example, the hymen. Derrida's deconstructional point of neither veil nor unveiling is a reference to Nietzsche's veil/unveil effect (*Schleier, Enthüllung, Verhüllung*) (see, for example, Derrida 1979: 51) of the truth as woman/woman as truth. So this becomes enfolded in Nietzsche's complex arguments about truth and illusion, and Heidegger's commentaries on this. In other words beyond the binarism of the doubling, is this style of thinking which flows on in the 'etc.' of such lists.

This is complex, and sometimes it can be frustrating, as the reader of Derrida must sometimes feel as if they are involved in a game of catch-up! However, we can make strong analytic use of this sensibility of beyond the double (as well as this seemingly unending flow of references across thinkers and texts). To work through it more clearly, and to consider how these ideas are useful for the study of visual cultures, we will look at two examples of critical reflexivity. The first of these, spectres, is something we find in a number of guises in Derrida's work. The second, mirrors, is perhaps more diffuse, but does offer an underpinning of some of the key concepts of deconstruction.

Visibility being eaten away: the spectre and the mirror

Let us play a sort of deconstructional game and use some of the terms from Derrida's list to define the status of spectres in texts. In a sense it goes against the spirit of the spirit because spectres should always resist positions. By its very definition the spectre inhabits a space that is neither living nor dead, neither present nor absent. So once we consider texts that attempt to represent spectres and spirits we encounter something that lies at the heart of the problems of representation noted above. Spectres even resist the middle ground between the transcendental and the sacrificial. And yet there is a sophisticated and extensive set of devices available to the film-maker and painter, photographer and dramaturge to show the spectre. Our examples will be drawn from cinema because in many ways that has become the main repository of spectral images in recent times.

The Sixth Sense (M. Night Shyamalan 1999) is a wonderfully deconstructive piece of cinema; not only in terms of the representation of spectres, but of cinema itself. The whole trick of the film works because it relies precisely on the conventions of representing spectres in films. The spectator never guesses (although of course there is always the chance he/she can) the truth about Malcolm Crowe because he breaks the rules of representing spectres – and besides we are too engaged in seeing the other spectres to notice his status. The boy, Cole, tells us he sees dead people, but we, like Malcolm, don't really listen and so allow him to become the third term. If the binary logic is applied (which it is) the spectator sees dead people (the spectres that hang from the rafters in the school, the woman on the bike, the boy who found his father's shot gun) and sees those who are still alive (the boy, his mother, the hundreds who pass across the screen). But the third term, the figure who breaks the binary opposition of dead and alive is Malcolm. And he does this because it is very difficult to think outside of the binarism, to think in terms of deconstructing opposites. Of course the catch in all of this is that the moment of revelation – when Malcolm and the spectator together realize he is in fact a spectre – the film retreats from its deconstructive turn and reinserts the binary opposition. It is as if only spectres and spectators can find (analytic) peace once the symmetry is reinscribed. Until this moment does take place, however, Malcolm operates as the pharmakon – neither remedy nor poison.

We see a similar game being played out in *The Others* (Amenábar 2001) where the mother refuses the status of death and the existence of spectres for herself and her children. They haunt themselves as much as they haunt the others (the living and the other spectres) until this status is resolved. Even so, in much the same way as Henry James' *The Turn of the Screw* (which this film seems to share an affinity with), the ending allows a certain amount of ambiguity as spectres move between worlds. Once more the whole premise behind the film's representation of spectres and the living is the refusal of a binary divide. In this example, to continue our comparison, if Malcolm demonstrates the pharmakon, Grace Stewart is like the hymen – neither consummation nor virginity, neither the veil nor unveiling.[12] And both visual representations work precisely because knowledge has been deconstructed.

These two spectres are recent examples, but the same sorts of things are illustrated in earlier film texts. *Psycho* (Hitchcock 1960) plays with a number of different sorts of deconstructions of the binary opposites through a different sort of spectre. Mother haunts Norman, and continues a shadowy sort of existence through him. As with Derrida's sense of the hymen, Mother is neither identity nor difference – she is neither Mother nor son, woman nor man, conscious nor unconscious. This is why at the same moment Mother is a form of identity (note it is more of a title than a name) and a difference to all forms of identity (no one called Mother actually exists – just a semi-mummified corpse and a vengeful force in Norman). A similar example, going back further in cinematic history, is Irene in *Cat People* (Tourneur 1942). Her existence as woman and cat, transforming from one to the other through a thinly disguised discourse of sexuality, operates beyond the binary divide of human/animal and more in the space beyond Western and non-Western, beyond Christianity and Paganism. Because she is represented so seductively (and with almost a sense of innocence) she works beyond the good/evil divide.

This status of Mrs Bates in *Psycho* reminds us of another version of the spectre in recent films. This is the slasher film, where the corporeal nature of the threat is often questionable. The figure of terror in these films (such as *Nightmare on Elm Street* (Craven 1984), *Friday the 13th* (Cunningham, 1980), *I Know What You Did Last Summer* (Gillespie 1997), *Scream* (Craven 1996)) has a very tangible aspect to it and quite often is not a spectre at all but linked to madness, urban legend, or revenge-driven loners. Yet these corporeally inscribed figures act as if they are spectres, moving across barriers (such as space and time) with seeming ease. They are part of the third term of the horror film because they can work the spaces of the living and the non-living. They question the rules of space, for example, by managing to leap out of areas they have no right to be in; they defy the rules of time because they continually emerge from the past (such as repression and histories) and threaten to operate in the future. In this way we can employ such figures to make sense of an aspect of *différance*. Derrida states: '*Différance* is what makes the movement of signification possible only if each element that is said to be "present", appearing on the stage of presence, is related to something other than itself but retains the mark of a past element and already lets itself be hollowed out by the mark of its relation to a future element' (Derrida 1973: 142). Derrida is aiming for something more than the serial killer, the evil in a slasher film, or the haunting spectres, but the status he is articulating does fit them. This idea that to operate in terms of *différance* is to necessarily contain within itself elements of the past and a possible future relation is what determines the threat of these figures. They must operate in terms of *différance* because the threat they bring is continually deferred and their status to others (the living) is always determined through difference.

This list of spectres and spirits can be continued, but the general sense should be fairly clear by now. It is interesting to note just how often cinema sets up the deconstruction of the status of spectre and living, but almost always feels it necessary to reinsert the binarism at the end of the film. This tends to show just how pervasive the binarism of Western thought is, and how difficult the deconstruction of it can be. Even in a genre such as the ghost story, which can betray its own rules and conventions, the return to resolve the status of the third term is quite compelling. Of course the deconstruction does not end at the conclusion of many of these films, particularly in the manifestation of the horror film since the 1980s. The flow of the horror genre is that even the dead can return – thus the resolved spectre can retain the status of coming back in a second, or indeed many subsequent, films.

It is also worth noting that Derrida himself engages in the figure and concept of the spectre. We see it extensively in *Spectres of Marx*, underpinning sections of *The Gift of Death*, and in key sections in *Politics of Friendship*. It is noteworthy (although once more we can only signal this here for it would take us too far from our main aim) that these are all central works in Derrida's writings on political philosophy. It is an interesting reflection on Derrida, perhaps, that when he engages in the political (something many have called on him to do for some time) there is an evocation of the spectral. However, even within this analysis of political philosophy by Derrida, much of the groundwork of deconstruction is to be found. Take, for example, the closing section of *Politics of Friendship* where Derrida is, once more, pursuing that ghostly figure of Nietzsche:

> A spectral distance would thus assign its condition to memory as well as to the future as such. The as such is affected with spectrality; hence is it no longer or not yet exactly what it is.
>
> (Derrida 1997: 288)

Derrida's description clearly relies on the sense of *différance* and time (see above), which is something we in turn have seen in terms of the cinema's representation of spectres and serial killers. For such figures rely precisely on this ambiguity of time – of living in memory and threatening the future. The *as such* of contemporary Hollywood films (middle-class, white suburbia) becomes affected by the spectrality of spectres, disfigured figures and tormented teenagers. Of course this is the domain of the horror genre – these are the same liminal figures of Frankenstein's monster, Heathcliff, the gothic images of demons and spirits, and so on.

There is one more feature of the spectre from Derrida that we need to consider before moving on to our related topic of mirrors. The spectral breaks down the opposition between self and other because it questions the processes employed to maintain those distinctions. In the horror and slasher film genres, the aspect that so often allows the threat to take place is the connection between the spectral and the central character (often a woman) – it is because of what she is that the figure from another realm can exist and continue to return. The spectral simultaneously challenges the order of spaces (and time) and asserts them (the white middle-class suburban world is defined as such because it contrasts so sharply with the world of spectres and mutilated killers). This means that the figure of the threat and potential victim become reflections of one another. One of the central themes in *Memoirs of the Blind* is the self-portrait, and Derrida figures this in quite a curious way. He argues that the extreme examination required in the self-portrait exerts a type of analysis quite unique in representation, and the consequence is one of ruin:

> Ruin is the self-portrait, this face looked at in the face as the memory of itself, what remains or returns as a specter from the moment one first looks at oneself and a figuration is eclipsed. The figure, the face, then sees its visibility being eaten away.
>
> (Derrida 1993: 68)

Apart from our recurring themes of the past and future, the other striking thing about this passage is that Derrida ties the self directly to a sort of spectralization. It is as if self-reflection is not possible unless it is inhabited by a spectre. This is because the self-portrait, like the spectral, contorts the sense of presence and absence, as well as the present and past/future.[13] The self-portrait, by its very nature, allows the vision of visibility to be eaten away. This takes us to the issue of mirrors.

MIRRORS

Hitchcock seemed to have an obsession with the mirror, for it can be spotted in so many of his films. *Spotted* because it is rarely focused on, just glanced at as the camera or character slides past it. Because they have this status of the almost unseen they resist one of the primary conventions of emphasis and meaning in Hollywood cinema. This is the idea that for something to have significance it must be shot in such a way that the spectator's gaze is drawn to it; the close-up, the zoom in, the return to the same shot are all examples of this. However, so many of Hitchcock's mirrors slide by and operate on a different level to the other events. One example is to be found in *Psycho* when Marion is shown in the motel room having a change of heart about the stolen money. Just before she takes her fateful shower the camera pans across the room and a mirror reflects the money. A simple image, but it contains within it all of the primary urges of the film: double dealings, doubled subjectivities, reflections on one's own position in life, and the returned gaze from potent objects.

Hitchcock's use of mirrors provides us with an interesting metaphor for philosophy and Derrida. Reflection is one of the cornerstones of philosophy – it is what philosophy defines itself as doing. There are whole systems of thought, and fiercely contested debates, about the degree and type of reflection (and in this is included reflexivity) that should be included in any system of thought.[14] It will take us too far away from our central issues here to engage too much in these histories and debates, but a final example will help locate much of what has already been discussed in this chapter. Our concern must be with how deconstruction operates in terms of the mirror – that is, the act of reflection. This is fundamentally about how Derrida attempts to get the philosophical discourses to reflect on themselves, and in so doing make us more reflexive in our approach to the ideas. Just as

Hitchcock's camera reveals and disguises the function of the mirror, so Derrida allows us to work within a moment of reflection. This is the tain, the 'behind', of the mirror that we do not see, but without it there can be no reflection of the image.

When we find moments of mirroring in an image there are a number of consequences that can occur. One is a sort of declaration of technique, a show within the image that such a thing can be done. Dutch still-life paintings are good examples of this, because what the tiny aspects of reflection (on bowls and jugs, cups and in water) perform is a sense of the life-like, but also a demonstration of the skill of the painter. In other words, we find combined within the single image both a denial of the artifice (the replication of the real) and a claim of it (the technique of the artist him/herself). Another possible consequence is that the whole discourse of the image is interrupted, perhaps even broken. These are the moments of reflection when the illusion of the text is arrested and the spectator is reminded that they are actually looking at something (which then returns their gaze). The direct address to the camera in cinema, the photographic moment that reveals the camera (the pseudo-sexuality of Helmut Newton's images,[j] for example, are so formulated that their sexuality becomes reflexive of a particular type (phallocentric) and era), and the use of mirrors in painting are all examples of this. Consider Van Eyck's *The Arnolfini Portrait*[k] that so effectively draws our eye beyond the two figures to the mirror between them. Here is the mirror that seems to hold both their world and the world of the spectator. This is a different sort of mirror to the one that dominates a great deal of painting, which is of the woman caught gazing at her own reflection.[15] This is a far more internalized reflexivity, taking up the spectator's role of looking at the pleasures of looking.

We refer to these images, and their processes of revealing technique and engaging in the act of spectating, because they illustrate a fundamental part of the deconstructionalist technique. They are textual forms that return us to the opening ideas in this chapter, for they have a certain parasitology attached to them. So often these mirrors do not sit on the same plane of existence as the rest of the objects in the image, but render visible, to be consumed by the spectator, the dynamics of the image. Deconstruction is the tain behind the ideas, drawing moments of reflection on the thing itself (be it an image or a definition of truth) and the participation of the spectator. 'Deconstruction,' says Derrida, 'does not consist in passing from one concept to another, but in overturning and displacing a conceptual order, as well as the non-conceptual order with which the conceptual order is articulated' (Derrida 1986: 329). All of the ideas we have looked at here – from mirrors and spectres to limits and viruses – are part of this process of overturning the conceptual order. By this we also mean how the image can be used in similar ways to overturn other orders, and the order of the visual in which it is itself located.

Notes

1 Derrida has noted on a number of occasions his surprise that deconstruction – a term he used within a string of terms – came to be a sort of catch-phrase for his work. The interview with him in *Positions* is interesting for this.

2 *Différance* is a term Derrida coined to emphasize the indeterminate nature of meaning and the interpretative act. It plays on the two meanings of difference and deferral. That is, argues Derrida, that all meanings are made up of acts of seeing differences; and because meaning is so slippery we are in a constant state of deferring the arrival at meaning.

3 Derrida also uses the theme of the parasite within a different context – that of painting – in *Memoirs of the Blind*. For example: '… you can hear them resonating all on their own, deep down in the drawing, sometimes right on its skin; because the murmuring of these syllables has already come to well up in it, bits of words parasiting it and producing interference' (Derrida 1993: 39). We shall return to this text later.

4 It would take us too far afield to work through the exchange between Lacan and Derrida on this issue. The reader can take up the issues further in the three key texts on this, namely Lacan's 'Seminar on "The Purloined Letter"', Derrida's *The Post Card*, and his paper 'For the Love of Lacan'. In passing the *letter en souffrance* are those letters that have failed to be delivered; and the additional meaning of *souffrance* – suffering – works particularly well for Lacan in his reading of the Poe short story and the anxiety of the Queen.

5 It is significant to recall the extensive analysis Derrida performs in much of his work on philosophers such as Heidegger, and how this has shaped much of deconstruction's methodology and subject matter. Heidegger's *Being and Time*, for example, is a text we see Derrida dealing with in many different situations. In this sense it is not surprising that time is an essential aspect to deconstruction.

6 This, of course, is one of the issues of measuring and tracking time. No event suddenly emerges, for there is always transition and change long before the manifestation. And yet we are shown events as if they mark a new order often out of the context of their histories.

7 See Derrida *Of Grammatology*, especially the section 'The Essay on the Origin of Languages'. Derrida's concerns are with Rousseau, and how the Enlightenment contributed to the idea of a centre that in effect produces meaning and a site for interpretation.

8 For a more detailed discussion of absence and Derrida see Fuery, *The Theory of Absence*.

9 It is interesting to note the story Derrida tells which led up to the staging of the exhibition. Derrida had been 'suffering for thirteen days from facial paralysis caused by a virus, from what is called *a frigore* (disfiguration, the facial nerve inflamed, the left side of the face stiffened, the left eye transfixed and horrible to behold in the mirror …)' (Derrida 1993: 32). This was two weeks of terror for him as he experienced a partial sense of blindness. It is not difficult to see the insertion of the personal that Derrida commences with, and continues with throughout the book.

10 Derrida writes on the impossibility of representation elsewhere. Of particular note is his piece 'Sending: On Representation' in Fuery 1995.

11 We can note a certain resonance in this idea with what is discussed in the chapter on Lacan as the third time. Both invite a position beyond the established, perhaps even beyond the comfortable.

12 It is somewhat accidental that these two examples have fallen the way they have – the male body of Bruce Willis used to illustrate the pharmakon – which Derrida explores through the body of Socrates; the female body of Nicole Kidman used to illustrate Nietzsche's and Derrida's points on woman as truth. But the genders do work in with the overall schema that Derrida develops in his works so perhaps it is best left in this way.

13 Here we are reminded of Barthes' sense of the *punctum* – which is the spectrely presence, and status, of the photograph. See the chapter on Barthes for further discussion of this.

14 An excellent summary of this situation, and Derrida's own position within it, is to be found in Rodolphe Gasché's *The Tain of the Mirror: Derrida and the Philosophy of Reflection*.

15 This links directly to the discussion on narcissism that is taken up in greater detail in the chapter on Lacan.

a Botticelli's Venus in *The Birth of Venus*
http://www.artchive.com/artchive/B/botticelli/venus.jpg.html

b Velázquez's Venus in *The Rokeby Venus*
http://www.artprints-on-demand.co.uk/noframes/velasquez/rokeby_venus.htm

c   Uma Thurman in *The Adventures of Baron von Munchhausen*
    http://www.imdb.com

d   Picasso's *Les Demoiselles d'Avignon*
    http://www.pbs.org/wgbh/cultureshock/flashpoints/visualarts/picasso_a.html

e   Van Gogh's *Pair of Boots*
    http://artprints-posters.com/artists/van_gogh/van_gogh.shtml

f   Damien Hirst – some examples
    http://dh.ryoshuu.com/art/1996someco.html
    http://dh.ryoshuu.com/art/1996partyt.html
    http://dh.ryoshuu.com/art/1996loving.html
    http://dh.ryoshuu.com/art/1991whenlo.html

g   Tracy Emin
    http://www.artseensoho.com/Art/LEHMANNMAUPIN/emin99/emin2.html

h   Robert Mapplethorpe
    http://www.mapplethorpe.org/selectedworks.html

i   Titian's *Danaé*
    http://www.geelonggallery.org.au/edu/students/conserve_.htm

j   Helmut Newton's images
    http://www.ionone.com/phtnewton.htm

k   Van Eyck, *The Arnolfini Portrait*
    http://www.nationalgallery.org.uk/cgi-
    bin/WebObjects.dll/CollectionPublisher.woa/wa/work?workNumber=NG186

Chapter Five

SPECTATOR, CULTURE, IMAGE ☐

Barthes and the visual

[T]he social formation is inherently and immanently present in the image and not a fate or external which clamps down on an image that might prefer to be left alone.[1]

How are images formed? What are their effects? How are images read, and what types of images are read by which demographics? The main concerns of this chapter look at the image in this way, focusing on how it is read within the parameters of visual cultures, predominantly, how an image comes to form an integral part of a visual culture (as well as possessing the ability to typify it) and how such a formulation shapes a visual culture. Instead of listing images and how they operate as individual examples, a more theoretical and conceptual approach will be taken, looking towards the role of the spectator and their influence on the image and in terms of the image. The relationships and interactions between spectator, culture and image will be looked at, and discussed with particular reference to the theories and works of Roland Barthes, to see how they form a fundamental basis for a visual culture. This chapter also seeks to outline the semiotics[2] of the image, and how the spectator's act of reading is crucial in the formation of the image, individually, and within a larger socio-cultural context. It is how the image is socially formed in which we are interested, and this type of questioning looks at the image's construction and capacity for signification.

The disciplines of visual cultures and visual theory are concerned with analysing the image, not as a single component within a specific field (such as art, for example), but instead examining the image as a concept operating within and from a wide range of media sources. The aim of this approach in thinking about the image is to look beyond its capacity for simple representation, and engage with all forms of image representation so that in considering the formation and function of the image, new concepts of images can emerge and help generate contemporary critical methods of interpretation. The aim of this chapter is to work towards a 're-modelling' or a 're-vision' of the image, looking at how it is formed, read and generates meaning in culture through analysing its structure, and then 'putting it back together' so that there is a different knowledge of the image and its place in visual cultures.

THE SPECTATOR AND CULTURE

The canvas: Roland Barthes

In this 're-structuring' of the image, it is necessary to scale back elements that combine to complete the final work in order to effectively figure their importance and relevance. All images begin with a blank 'canvas': literally, such as a blank page, empty book, blank computer screen, grey cinema screen, grey television set; or metaphorically, such as empty social space, lack of cultural expression. It is this metaphorical sense of the blank canvas that we are using in looking at Roland Barthes' theories on signification and how signs possess meaning, to help us to systematically work through the formation of the image in culture, not as an artist paints it, or author writes it, or director directs it, but how the image, as a system of signification, comes to hold meaning in socio-cultural discourses. The elements of the image we will look at deal more with the position of the image, its effect and how culture fits in with the image and vice versa, rather than the artistic elements of an image, such as paintwork, or acting, or even the technical composition of the image.

Primarily, Barthes was not concerned with the 'end meaning' of a text – he would argue that there is no such thing – but he was interested in how its potential for production and possession of meaning is realized. Barthes was interested in how we make sense of texts, what it is about them that allows us to make meaning of them to ourselves, to others and to culture. Using literature as his example, Barthes focused on viewing a text not as a portrayal of something or a symbol, rather he viewed the text as a sequence of codes that 'Literature' produced, and looked at how these operated as literary works and their place and relevance in the discursive practice of culture. Applying this system of thought to the image is problematic in that it is hard to separate the issue of representation from the image given the cultural codes and discourses through which we have been trained to interpret them. However, what Barthes' structuralist mode of thought does (and this can include the image) is shift the focus of our interpretation, directing it away from any controlled form of interpretation and towards the codes that order the image's meaning. It is almost as if we should conceive of the image as nothing else but a systematic mass of complex and intricate socio-cultural relations that have been ordered in very specific ways to produce a variety of meanings. To illustrate this approach we can turn to the specific visual example of colour.

In the Tate Modern gallery, London, there hangs a piece by Yves Klein. It is a single square canvas painted in monochrome blue, one of around 200 blues that Klein 'created'. Its title is its colour *IKB 79*[a], *IKB* standing for International Klein Blue, the number referring to its position in the sequence. On one level the image appears to ask: 'What do you think I represent?' or to question, 'Guess what I represent.' Its immediate engagement with the spectator begins on the level of representation and seemingly initiates a discourse in this vein. After all, aren't we conditioned to see 'art' or 'the image' as representative of higher or more obscure meaning? To engage with the blue square on this interpretative level, however, is to miss its function and social place as an image in the Tate Modern and as an image overall. What this blue square entitled *IKB 79* does is to re-present and attempt to generically subvert the systems and network of relations that are often used by spectators to 'decipher' an image. The blue square asks to be read as a conscious image, through its self-reflexive positioning, and seeks a critical interpretation from its spectators. By only being a blue square, the image calls into question the arbitrary nature of signification. It cheekily states that a blue square represents nothing, but actually re-presents cultural conception of 'the image' so that a spectator re-views it, aware of its reliance and comment on cultural codes regarding the interpretation of images in general. Symbolism and its employment are questioned – how can a blue square symbolize anything? Yet in creating a new colour (and subsequently drawing attention to the use of colour and its place within culture and within visual cultures) – Klein's 79th version – what is emphasized is the social formation of the image as a web of cultural codes and arbitrary systems, socially formed through such relations. Klein also clearly makes room for, indeed almost depends on, the spectator's conscious and critical act of reading, as central to such a formation. As a result, *IKB 79* not only challenges and disrupts the system of, and social response to representation, but also uncovers the arbitrariness of colour that has been ordered to produce specific spectator positions and responses.

From this metaphorical blank canvas we are interested in seeing how these relations are formed, ordered and combined to produce meaning. One point of departure in discussing these relations is to consider Barthes' questioning approach towards signification. Barthes' methodology of examining the 'how' and 'why' regarding a text's meaning was a new mode of thinking and his influence here for the image is not the extrapolation of a text's 'end' absolute meaning but to question its *potential* for meaning – its capacity to culturally signify meaning in specific discourses. Even though for a large part of Barthes' work literature was his main focus, his essays on photography, cultural icons and images all debate a similar concern – how does the structure of a text contribute to their meaning? In *Camera Lucida* (1984), Barthes moves closer towards analysing the image and talks of the photograph and its eidetic qualities. 'The Photograph gives a little truth, on condition that it parcels out the body. But this truth is not that of the individual, who remains irreducible; it is the truth of lineage' (Barthes 1984: 103). Barthes is aware that any interpretation of the Photograph has the danger of relying on similar interpretative paradigms of the text. 'Photography's Referent is not the same as the referent of other systems of representation. I call "photographic referent" not the *optionally* real thing to which an image or a sign refers but the *necessarily* real thing which has been placed before the lens' (Barthes 1984: 76). Part of Barthes' discussion in *Camera Lucida* is focused on the machinations and cultural weight of the Photograph, as well as his working through his grief for his late mother. His comments on the Winter Garden photograph recognize this 'reality' that is present in photographs and absent in other images. Barthes here is distinguishing between the Photograph as a mechanistic technical apparatus possessing a cultural currency from the individual photograph.

For Barthes, the Photograph resides wholly in culture, and in Part One of *Camera Lucida* he reads the photographic image in terms of his pleasure as a spectator and, in Part Two, analyses the nature of the photograph through and in spite of such pleasure. Barthes is looking at his late mother's photos, and photos of her. For him these particular photos give a truth that is found in the network of relations that form the social discourse present and recognizable between Mother and Son. We can only read about Barthes-as-spectator in terms of these photos of his mother, but in doing so, we can view how these images and how they signify are formed through this particular socio-discursive practice existing between family members, here Mother and Child. He discusses his feelings for his mother, and in part, works through his grief of loss through the image, displaying that a large part, if not all, of the formation of the structure of an image occurs through the act of reading.

What this discussion of the photograph also indicates is just how central the image has become in culture. It is important to recognize that how we as spectators view the image is largely invested in the identification of images, working along their sequences (their placement in culture, the chain of relations that contextualize them) as well as suggest other images that can signify the same meanings as the originally viewed image. A good example of this is found in *Camera Lucida*, where Barthes inserts a photograph by Nadar called *The Artist's Mother (or Wife)*.[b] Barthes has been discussing the photos of his late mother, 'There I was, alone in the apartment where she had died, looking at these pictures of my mother, one by one, under the lamp, gradually moving back in time with her, looking for the truth of the face I had loved. And I found it' (Barthes 1984: 67). This positioning of Nadar's photograph 'in' Barthes' reminiscing illustrates how an image comes to signify through a social formation of a particular discursive practice. For the reader/spectator it does not matter that this is not Barthes' mother, as in conjunction with Barthes' story, the spectator identifies the image as relevant to the text[3] and Barthes' personal narrative, purely based on its textual placement.

The image is underscored with a quotation, 'Who do you think is the world's greatest photographer? Nadar', as well as the name of the photograph and the artist (Barthes 1984: 68). The photograph *is* momentarily Barthes' mother as the discourse and structure of illustrated stories is a familiar one. By placing the photo at this point in *Camera Lucida*, Barthes plays with the construction of the image and the link between word and image by identifying the modes through which an image comes to signify. He uses culturally familiar and accessible discursive practices for the reader to recognize and engage with. These are the discourse of grief – looking over old photos of a lost loved one to remember past events and relive fond memories, and the discourse of the familial structure, here Mother and Child. This structure of social relations and practices helps Barthes to emphasize his point that each photograph (and any subsequent interpretation) is individual and yet related within a code. Further, Barthes hints at the pleasure the spectator derives from associating with the photograph in this way, but we will speak more about pleasure later in the chapter. As a side note, this practice of inserting images to visually substantiate text is dominant in all forms of media, particularly news bulletins where a picture of the narrated story functions as 'anchor' in the top right-hand corner, not necessarily taken at the same time.

Nadar's photo is of an old woman with grey hair and it is tempting to interpret her as Barthes' mother, even though we are told that she isn't. This highlights how the image and representation easily slip from the specific to the universal, which is part of the identification of the image and how we can recognize the image's position in relation to culture (the codes that recognize this is a valid representation of an old woman – a possible mother of someone) and in relation to other photographs (photographs of the same era and fashion). This photograph operates on a similar level to Foucault's analysis (*This is not a Pipe* 1983b) of Magritte's paintings *The Treachery of Images* (1928/29) and *The Two Mysteries*^c (1966).[4] In these two paintings the statement *Ceci n'est pas une pipe* (This is not a pipe) appears under a drawing of a pipe. The representation of a pipe is obviously not a real pipe, but in painting such a statement Magritte calls to attention the reality of objects and the tension between that reality and the image. His painted statement illustrates the investment of trust in the written word over the image, yet at the same time also illustrates the spectator's desire to resist that the pipe in the painting is not a pipe. As with Nadar's photo, 'this is not a mother' and, more precisely, 'this is not Barthes' mother', but as spectators we desire to read it as such. We will come to more of Barthes' work on the act of reading and its significance in the shaping of a text's meaning later.

In figuring out what is the metaphorical blank canvas of the image, we are questioning its social fabric – how the image fits into culture and what becomes a part of the image's structure. The image is a system – a social construction of cultural etiquette, rules and dogma, and Barthes's influence is felt primarily in this analysis of such a system. The spectator's critical responsibility in viewing the image is not to 'guess' or discover its intended meaning, as this is a passive stance suggesting that all meaning 'within' an image is predetermined. Rather the spectator needs to assume an active role and interpret the visual image as a cultural product, identifying its place in the system of visual production and significance in culture. The spectator should not engage with the image as a detective hoping to solve its mystery, but from a critical perspective, seeking to discover why the image signifies what it does, and how it holds the capacity to do so. By working from this position, the spectator analytically looks beyond the primary level of the image (its surface) and sees it as a cultural invention, formed through definite social discursive structures.

SEMIOTICS OF THE IMAGE

Narrative structures

The image is continually being located as a culturally formed structure of social discourse. To comprehend this particular capacity and operation of the image, and its high significance in culture, images need to be 're-viewed' – that is, seen outside of their normal functioning. Viewed in this way images, and systems of images, begin to disrupt, jar and disturb static viewing positions, and are removed from their intended purpose, which is to go unquestioned and remain as unseen, 'natural' aspects of culture. Part of Barthes' influence stems from his structuralist theories, which regarded social and cultural phenomena as exchange commodities resulting from arbitrary systems such as language. Working from this position, Barthes viewed everything that exists in culture as a product. His main premise is that these cultural artifices (images, texts, landmarks, architecture) have no essence – there is nothing natural about them, yet throughout the myriad of relations that construct their meaning, they can appear as a most natural part of culture.

In order to analyse how these artifices generate meaning, Barthes argued that it was necessary to closely assess the systems that combined in order to make the signification possible. Barthes was particularly interested in how these systematic relations constantly intertwined to form meaning, and how the structure of these relations operated in specific socio-cultural discourses. In order to 'reveal' these arbitrary structures of signification, Barthes turned to linguistic and literary fields to analyse how literary structures were formed: 'The critic is not responsible for reconstructing the work's message but only its system' (Barthes 1964: 256). Barthes analysed works from literature (predominantly of the late nineteenth century, including Balzac, Flaubert, Proust, and some avant-garde writers such as Robbe-Grillet) using linguistic theory in order to separate and distinguish the structures of relations that formed the 'literariness' of these literary works.

While aspects of such an analysis were fruitful for Barthes, it is harder to apply a linguistic analysis to the image, especially as the written language, if present, is usually minimal or at the very most, an element of resistance and ambiguity.[5] In interpreting the image, however, there is a form of reading. As spectators, we attempt to engage with the image in similar ways to how we engage with written text – we do try to discover its meaning as culture, and society has established the discursive practice that 'Art' means something, or that an artist is trying to convey a 'feeling' or some such other ethereal thought. We ask 'What does it mean?' or 'What is it trying to say/convey?' Our interest with meaning has not abated and Barthes' further work on analysing narrative and narrative structures helps us understand our spectator's obsession with the meaning of an image. What forms a narrative? What types of combination produce different narratives? Why is applying narrative structure to an image such a desirable, and compulsive thing to do? And why are some narratives chosen over others as possessing higher cultural importance and significance? These are the sorts of questions that Barthes tried to answer through analysing narratives.

In a number of essays collected as *Image-Music-Text* (1977), Barthes carries out a variety of structural analyses of narrative. He develops a semiotic methodology to systematically uncover the way in which structure generates meaning. This approach allows Barthes to critically interpret discourses as systems and parts of larger discourses, working through how networks of relations are combined to form meanings.

> Narrative is first and foremost a prodigious variety of genres, themselves distributed amongst different substances – as though any material were fit

to receive man's stories. Able to be carried by articulated language, spoken or written, fixed or moving images, gestures, and the ordered mixture of all these substances ... narrative is present in every age, in every place, in every society; it begins with the very history of mankind and there nowhere is nor has been a people without narrative.

(Barthes 1977: 79)

In questioning narrative and its function, Barthes argues that one of structuralism's main concerns should be to determine the multiple fragments that constitute a text and work towards a definition of the 'language' through which they are read. The aim was to develop a form of technique in analysing narrative systems and structures, that would help find a common structure that grouped these systems/discourses together within a text to produce a narrative. Barthes acknowledged that narrative structures were heterogeneous in their receivership and their production, and realized that each narrative should be analysed individually to uncover its own unique structure. However, Barthes argued against a predetermined 'author' that could clarify or completely answer any questions or meaning from the narrative. Barthes went on to analyse the effect of such techniques through various groupings of narrative structures, using examples from French culture.

In 'The Eiffel Tower' (1979), Barthes uses the French cultural icon, the Eiffel Tower, to critique its narrative importance and placement (both physical and social) in French culture. His reading and analysis of the tower's presence and effect on the French people uncovers its visual importance as a cultural structure through interpreting and discussing its literal signification.

The Tower is not a usual spectacle; to enter the tower, to scale it, to run around its courses, is, in a manner both more elementary and more profound, to accede to a view and to explore the interior of an object (though an openwork one).

(*A Roland Barthes Reader*, 1993: 240)

The Tower is climbed as a signifier of France so that upon reaching the first or second level, one gets a bird's eye view of French quintessence, Paris. From this position, the viewer can see the environs of Paris and because of the force of the cultural signifiers, he or she is aware that the building, people, parks, traffic and river they are seeing connote '*Frenchness*'. In other words, we do not simply see a city but rather we see strongly connotative signs. Just as Barthes examines a structure embedded in French culture to highlight its narrative formation and function, the visitor to the Tower uses its structure, both as a literal construction out of metal and other man-made material, and as an abstract man-made construction out of cultural discourse and propaganda, to systematically uncover the method through which another structure (Paris) generates meaning (what typifies '*Frenchness*'). The Eiffel Tower as it stands, functions *as an image* rather than a building apparatus because of such cultural signification. It is because of its national and international ubiquity that the Eiffel Tower is more than a lookout over Paris, more than a Parisian landmark, and more than a tourist must-see. This avenue of thought leads us to another aspect of Barthesian influence for the image – cultural narrative.

Cultural narratives and the image

Barthes' driving concern lies with the systems and structures in cultural discourses that seemingly move from mythical invention to natural fact. These systems and structures create and sustain socio-cultural discourses, which in turn, form cultural narratives. But what are cultural narratives? Looking at cultural narratives is a field of study in itself, so for our purposes here we will look at their importance and formation briefly, and what relevance they possess in terms of the image. The term 'cultural narratives' is used to describe and identify the way culture represents or expresses itself, and the narrativizing of culture. It is usually done so via any expressive medium, either visual, such as film, television, art, literature, or aural – music, radio, etc. Culture constructs narratives from networks of relations, from discourses and from any aspect that exists within its society so that eventually these arbitrarily chosen signifiers are synonymous with the culture (again, the Eiffel Tower is a good example of this). These relations can include such discourses as fashion, nationality, colour, buildings, voice, food, art, nature and animals to literally form a 'story'. An example of an Australian cultural narrative presented visually can be found in the television personality Steve Irwin, the 'Crocodile Hunter'.[6] Steve's persona is a creation and expression of a particular side of Australian culture and lifestyle, and part of this process is a visual cultural narrative.

Barthes' works are important here because it is his methodology of critically interpreting narrative structures that helps us see how the visual becomes invested with, and in, cultural narrative. In Steve Irwin we can find a network of relations that have combined to produce a representation of Australian culture. His costume (khaki workwear, unruly hairstyle, work boots) signifies the hard-working man of Australia in natural settings (hence the khaki colouring of his shirt and shorts) – a person connected to the land, as if most white Australians are of this ilk, which they aren't. Attached to his costume is Steve's line of work: hands-on, rough wrestling with nature and its dangerous creatures. Just with these two simple extractions from what is Steve Irwin, we can note how a combination of discourses (such as fashion and nature) help to establish a network of relations that contribute towards the formation of a narrative structure and subsequently, a cultural narrative. The more the television personality Steve Irwin is circulated through the visual medium, the more his image will become synonymous with the Australian culture and way of life. At present, his character is a part of the American *Sesame Street* ensemble, indicating that this has, in part, already happened.

Further examples of how the visual is invested with cultural narrative can also be found through advertisements. In *Image-Music-Text*, Barthes analyses an advertisement for Panzani pasta, with the aim of answering the issue – do images 'produce true systems of signs and not merely simply agglutinations of symbols?' (Barthes 1977: 32). Here Barthes looks at the pasta advertisement and assembles it into three messages with the aim of uncovering its total structure.[7] While Barthes systematically looks at the advertisement through these three messages (linguistic, denoted and connoted messages) what he is essentially doing is attempting to locate this image as a visual cultural narrative in a socio-specific culture and context. He works through the formation of the image (the three messages working like layers) to discover what enables the spectator to read it and engage with visual cultural narrative. How any sense is formed of an image of 'some packets of pasta, a tin, a sachet, some tomatoes, onions, peppers, a mushroom, all emerging from a half-open string bag, in yellows and greens on a red background' (Barthes 1977: 33), relies on how this typology of image is dealt with in France *in general* and also in other cultural contexts. Even though Barthes is a Frenchman reading an advertisement in France, part of his sorting-through of his three messages is applicable to all cultures as a visual sense exists everywhere for every spectator – this is the formation of cultural narrative through the visual. From here we can say that part of the formation of a visual cultural narrative incorporates this concept of a 'visual sense' – but how is this formed and where does one get it?

Visual sense moves the spectator closer to the image through recognition of cultural identity and performance. In Barthes' Panzani pasta advertisement, the colours that have been chosen are specifically Italian, and the foodstuffs represent Italian food. However, these meanings are only produced visually as they depend on knowledge of the Italian flag, and through this knowledge is recognition of the ideologies and practices of Italian culture. With this type of visual example it is easy to see how stereotypes are formed and maintained. Even though Barthes' example is taken from the 1960s, there is surprisingly consistent recurrence of these techniques in advertising; take, for example, the advertisement for Tommy perfume. Here we have the colours red, white and blue on the label of the perfume and in the combination of the costumes of the young, good-looking people, smiling and laughing in the promotional campaign. The visual sense of this advertisement is the same as that of the Panzani ad. The colours are representative of the American flag and also reflect the ideologies of American culture – freedom, happiness and prosperity. Buy Panzani pasta and you will buy fresh food and eat like Italians, buy Tommy cologne/perfume and you will be a free spirit, happy and healthy. These same sorts of issues occur not only in advertisements; Delacroix's painting *Liberty Leading the People* is famous for its striking image of revolution and popular uprising. Placed throughout the painting are patches of red, white and blue (for example, on the clothes of the people, in the sky in the background), working visually in the same manner as the pasta and perfume advertisements. Investing in cultural narratives via the visual in these ways helps to shape a spectator's subjectivity, ideology and ultimately a culture's consciousness.

Punk as cultural narrative

Maintaining this critical practice and view of the image in visual culture, we can look at how images, even the most abstract examples, are constructed through systems and structures such as cultural narratives to produce certain meaning at certain times and for certain effect. The image has become a powerful aspect of culture, not just through its cultural omnipresence but also through its ability to contribute to, respond to and in some cases ignite, political change.

Some examples are found in, but not limited to, the art works of Warhol, Peter Greenaway films, *Kramer vs Kramer* (Benton 1979), and Lynch's *Blue Velvet* (1986), *Elephant Man* (1980); in television programmes such as *The League of Gentlemen* (Bendelack 1999), *The Prisoner* (Markstein *et al.* 1967) and *A TV Dante* (Greenaway and Phillips 1989); and finally in photographs, particularly the photographs produced as postcards. Punk is an apt example of how a visual cultural narrative can be politically and culturally powerful. The significance of punk in the 1970s is structurally different both in terms of its objective realities (being fashion and hairstyles, etc.) and its active realities (being rebellion through protest or other forms) to the re-presentation of punk in the new millennium.

Viewing the image of punk as an example of visual culture highlights how the ontology of an image is a structure of socio-cultural networks, possessing signification based on the cultural moment wherein they present themselves. Today you can buy a postcard of a person with a punk hairstyle in London, or see David Beckham's 2002 punk-esque hairstyle, and these represent an appropriation of the punk rebellion, either as a position in the fashion system, or as a representative of a particular culture. Whilst they do not carry the same culturally disruptive meanings as the punk of the 1970s, they symbolize the time that it was disruptive and how their meaning, both then and now, is totally dependent on a network of relations that are unstable, especially where cultural attitude is paramount. An example of how these networks of relations come to form meaning can be found in the cultural narrative of punk. Aesthetically, Sid Vicious operated as a synecdoche for the 1970s punk movement. His hair, clothing, voice and performance combined to produce a visual cultural narrative of punk, at the very least 'what punk looked like'. His non-conformist hairstyles (signifier), rebellion, anti-establishmentarianism (signified) produce the signification of sub-cultural political expression – so that every multi-coloured mohawk or other punk appearance seen in the 1970s became a part of the network of relations that meant 'punk'.

Similarly, David Beckham's punk-esque hairstyle at the 2002 World Cup can be read in this way: recognized as a punk hairstyle, then as fashion, to be interpreted not as a homage but as cutting edge. As punk was also a significantly London phenomenon, it also signifies Britishness on the level of fashion. All combine, in a similar manner and to similar effect, as a narrative structure, to form, support and reinforce the cultural *zeitgeist* of these images. This interpretation and recognition of Beckham's punk hairstyle is formed through the recognition of the visual cultural narratives of punk in the 1970s and the post-1970s de-politicized (semi-parodical) version of punk.

Re-viewing the canvas: recognizing codes

Part of the operation and processes of narrative structures is the recognition of and subscription or resistance to codes, either literary, visual, cultural or a combination of these. In forming the systems and structures that construct meaning, codes are the primary structures in making certain signs more meaningful than others. As a result, despite the potential each sign has for meaning, the code through which it/they are read by, limits, as well as expands, this potential. Codes also operate like borders, photo frames, television screens, and margins, in that they 'frame' the possibilities that are present for interpretation. A useful example of this is genre. In *The Texas Chainsaw Massacre* (Hooper 1974), a spectator's interpretation is commonly based on fear and fright, whereas in Wes Craven's *Scream* trilogy (1996, 1997, 2000), the same signs are used to denote horror but the code through which they are read is altered. Consequently, the film is humorous and self-reflexive, as well as scary.

This is another aspect of a code's function – the preference for certain signs over others. Magritte's *The Treachery of Images* (1929), as discussed in the chapter on Foucault, shows how the code of viewing a painting is different to the code of reading a sentence. Which code allows these signs to mean *and* to dominate? There is no predetermined answer to this question but it highlights that this element of formation in a code is an integral part in the act of reading any text. Here the spectator/reader has the possibility to conform, resist and/or exploit the preferred signs in a code. Any choice that is made here is a response to the code's fundamental contribution in the construction of meaning, that being the system through which the signs are combined and structured. Barthes was interested in the *effect* of these codes and how their systematic structuring creates meanings for some signs over others, and how the act of reading constructs meaning from these signs. From a structuralist perspective, these meanings (for Barthes, literary meanings) are formed and generated by recognized codes within socio-cultural discourses, such as the time lapse between edited shots in film, or between commercial breaks in a television programme. Even a static time frame lapse, one example is in Frederick McCubbin's triptych *The Pioneer* (1904),[d] is accepted and understood by the spectator and quietly remains an inconsequential element in the readership of this image. Barthes' agenda was to 'strip down' these codes, and question the cultural moments where they remain unquestioned and are referred to as 'natural'.

One avenue that Barthes argues achieves this is through the role of the reader (for our purposes here, the spectator) and their active interpretation of a text, questioning its place in the network of cultural relations, including their own position. The spectator produces meaning through their acts of reading (interpretation) that conform, resist and/or exploit the narrative structure of an image. For Barthes, a text's meaning is shaped by the act of reading, which positions it and locates it within culture. The 'opening up' of the text, the viewing of the image, is what designates its meaning and its relationship to culture. Barthes coins two terms to denote these acts of reading: the readerly and the writerly. Remembering that Barthes was arguing for a 'stripping down' of codes to expose their 'naturalness', the importance of these terms lies in their creativity.

What this means for the spectator of the image is that the images themselves are not writerly or readerly, but rather it is the act of reading the image that contributes to its meaning. An aspect that it is important to emphasize is that although Barthes empowers the reader as a person with conscious responsibility in reading a text, it is a role in response to and in interaction with a text that he is outlining.

> The 'I' [spectator/reader] which approaches the text is already itself a plurality of other texts, of codes which are infinite or, more precisely, lost (whose origin is lost). Objectivity and subjectivity are of course forces which can take over the text, but they are forces which have no affinity with it ... Yet reading is not a parasitical act ... It is a form of work ... I am not hidden within the text, I am simply irrecoverable from it: my task is to move, to shift systems whose perspective end neither at the text nor at the 'I'.
>
> (Barthes 1974: 10)

So for the image, and ultimately visual cultures, it is within the spectator's act of viewing, and subsequent interpretation, where meanings are formed. As this engagement between spectator and image takes place, the act of viewing becomes an addition of a visual culture. This is the case even though the spectator may not have seen a particular image before. They will have seen other images, likewise or not. As a result, acts of viewing are the primary elements of visual culture because of this accumulation of images and knowledges about them, and ways of viewing. In short, this is the way we become visually literate.

THE ACT OF READING AND THE FORMATION OF THE TEXT

The rise of the image

Barthes writes that there is no more a destructive process of one voice or one origin than the act of writing.[8] In earlier times, when writing was one of the most dominant forms of media, this was a plausible claim. However, today media is dominated by images, leaving words and writing to supplement the image as a structural support or as an invitation into the meaning of the image. Our cultural and individual eye gravitates towards the picture on the front page of the newspaper before the stories outlining and explaining what the picture *is*; gravitates towards the stars in the film poster before looking to see what the film is about; and this is because within the image, we have already surmised and read enough to be basically informed, the writing completes the image. We can recognize instantly what code the image is to be read by, and use the writing that surrounds it for further interpretation and reinforcement of these codes. To interpret the image only in this practice however is limiting as it constantly requires the need to return to an authorial figure and negate, or at the very least, reduce, the involvement of the reader/spectator in the formation of the text's meaning.

In Barthes' famous article, 'The Death of the Author', he argues that writing is an active process, splintering and rupturing any possible link to an author whose intention is absolute. 'We know now that a text is not a line of words releasing a single "theological" meaning (the "message of the Author-God") but a multi-dimensional, space in which a variety of writings, none of them original, blend and clash' (Barthes 1977: 146). Barthes uses the dichotomy of author/reader to illustrate how writing is a highly developed process employed to disrupt the codes, systems and structures that are put in place to produce and interpret it. For Barthes, it is the issue of interpretation that he is arguing against, and he uses the author as figurehead to illustrate how interpretation (and the codes that direct it) is a product of culture and its narratives. To invest too much into Barthes' claim 'the birth of the reader must be at the cost of the death of the author' (Barthes 1977: 148) is to completely miss his argument and fall into the trap of investing in interpretation, although it is necessary to understand his reasons for this claim and why such a misunderstanding is easy to make.

On the surface, Barthes' argument appears succinct and not too difficult a concept to follow – the author doesn't exist, rather it is the reader who forms meaning and who can understand a text's meaning. This view or 'interpretation' is simplistic and merely inverts Barthes' thesis, turning the reader into a type of author. In giving 'birth to the reader', Barthes is recognizing the potential in readership to be rebellious, and also recognizes the seduction of constructing an authorial figure in the interpretative process. He acknowledges that there is significant pressure and emphasis within culture to 'seek the truth' in a text and kills the author as an example, but at the same time does not want to re-create one in a reader. What Barthes is aiming for is the opportunity for multiple voices to emerge from a text, along with multiple readership positions. The 'birth of the reader' is not simply the birth of one reader but a concept that allows every text to be freed from the focus of interpretation, or reverence to an author. The birth of the reader is a critical birth, an invitation extended to all readers of all texts to 're-view' a text outside of the cultural established and reinforced codes of interpretation.

Whilst many of Barthes' theoretical examples relied on literary resources, there are references to the image indicating that his theories are applicable to and rich for any visual medium. Barthes cites Surrealism in an attempt to demonstrate that investing in an author is to invest in interpretation. Surrealism, briefly defined here, is a 'subversion of codes', and one of its tangents was automatic writing where the writer would write whatever came into his/her head, writing as fast as possible. Barthes uses this branch of Surrealism for a number of reasons, but mainly to acknowledge that there is no real possibility of disregarding codes but a potential to exploit them exists, and is realized through the disavowal of seeking the text's 'truth' either through the author or any other means. 'Once the Author is removed, the claim to decipher a text becomes quite futile. To give a text an

Author is to impose a limit on that text, to furnish it with a final signified, to close the writing' (Barthes 1977: 147). To avoid this interpretative gesture on the part of the reader, Barthes argued that writing was a heterogeneous process and exercise, and in order to gain or understand the importance and relevance of writing demands a similar approach in readership. By inviting readers or spectators to involve themselves with a text in this manner, Barthes opened all facets of writing – its voice, its words, its construction and its deliverance. This re-thinking of writing is influential for the image as it gives spectators a level from which to 're-view' and 're-involve' themselves with the image. This is the birth of the spectator.

The birth of the spectator is the fundamental point from which the spectator views the image, and indeed any interaction with visual cultures overall, as a creative process. What unfolds in the viewing of the image is a questioning act that allows the spectator to view the image differently – outside the set boundaries of authorial discourse. In this critical mode of thought, we can view the image through other means rather than the simple outlining and discussion of, for example, aesthetics. The image is a series of systems, a structure of discourses and codes endorsing either a moment or *zeitgeist* of a particular culture and society. This is in part how some images get chosen over others in terms of popularity or for depicting realism, and how the forms of the image are categorized. An example being why da Vinci's *Mona Lisa* retains a canonical (high-art) position in culture and Duchamp's *L.H.O.O.Q.* (Reproduction of the Mona Lisa of Leonardo da Vinci with Moustache and Beard Added in Pencil)[c] (1920) disrupts that canonicity but creates one of its own. For Barthes this active engagement with a text, this critical birth, is only ever about uncovering the relation of systems and structures, working in and against codes, critically assessing discourses to uncover the potential for meaning and how it occurs: 'In the multiplicity of writing [the visual], everything is to be disentangled, nothing deciphered; the structure can be followed, 'run' (like the thread of a stocking) at every point and at every level, but there is nothing beneath' (Barthes 1977: 147). This is a good point to look at these codes in depth and see how they fit in with the spectator, culture and the image.

Fragments and codes

In *S/Z* (1974) Barthes stipulates the five codes through which cultural codes are grouped via certain signifiers. They consist of the hermeneutic code, which is the code that orders the signifiers and subsequently the interpretation of meaning; the semic code, which, as Barthes puts it, 'we merely indicate them ... we allow them the instability, the dispersion, characteristic of motes of dust, flickers of meaning' (Barthes 1974: 19), they are the elements within culture, whether it be an image or another text, that hold no meaning but have meaning attached to them, such as stereotypes, that help the spectator form an interpretation – like understanding the time lapse in television programming from commercial to commercial. Barthes specifies the symbolic code to identify the superficiality of the grouping of signifiers, and subsequently the investment of meaning in any particular sign. This code helps to sketch out the idea that any ordering of the image is an arbitrary one whether it is an internal ordering, such as interpreting the elements of the image (for example, Freud's couch[f] in relation to his study and analyst chair) or an external ordering (locating what the couch signifies in the larger order of psychoanalysis – such as its foundation). The proairetic code distinguishes sequential features of interpreting an image. We look at Freud's couch and we list the plush rug that covers it, the cushions that *make it look* comfortable, and we go on listing these items as though they were items on a shopping list, helping us form the connotative meanings associated with the couch – those that are not visually present but that depend on the visual in order to exist – for example, the practice of psychoanalysis where, Freud acts as a cultural icon that represents a particular vein of psychoanalysis and that represents a key figure in twentieth-century thought. These things cannot be seen by looking at Freud's couch in his London study (his real one), but by combining these codes with Barthes' last code, the referential code, we can formulate such typologies of cultural meaning. The referential code is cultural information, 'the cultural codes are references to a science or body of knowledge; in drawing attention to them, we merely indicate the type of knowledge referred to' (Barthes 1974: 20).

Another example of this sort of reading of invisibilities is the voice. Barthes discusses what he terms the grain of the voice, which is that exquisite effect of the voice as it brings *jouissance* to the listener. More than this, the grain is 'the body in the voice as it sings, the hand as it writes, the limb as it performs' (Barthes 1977: 188). This grain is achieved, read and understood, through the five codes. Its 'visuality' is to be understood as we take up each of the codes to feel its pleasure, as well as locate it within a cultural context. An example will help to clarify this. When Buffy talks in a high-pitched, disjointed manner, the viewer draws on cultural information and stereotypes of what represents and typifies femininity, in this case American teenage femininity located within a particular class and social domain.[9] Her tone and speech patterns construct vulnerability that further associates her as a 'good' slayer, adhering to and operating within the ideology of the righteous, fighting for truth, justice and the American way.

These five codes, according to Barthes, help to collate the fragments of meaning in any text, structure them and interpret them as though they were 'natural' aspects of culture. In approaching these images as a critical spectator, in the vein that Barthes intended, it is possible to perceive the heterogeneity of the image at the same time as acknowledging the codes they are structured by. The avenue that visual cultures invite us to take therefore, is one of unravelling and not translation. Each image or collation of images, even a genre of film can be read in this way so that this position of spectatorship helps to form, or using Barthes' words, give birth to, various visual cultures.

READER AND CREATION OF THE IMAGE

The spectator and visual culture

When we think of the image and its place within a visual culture it is often in terms of a static representation such as the photograph, the painting, the sketch, the drawing, and the cartoon (although this has a sense of continuing movement in its strip). Other forms of image such as the cinematic and televisual are usually typified in terms of their presentation – as *moving* images – like a connected but separate existence of the image. Indeed even architecture presents us with fragmented and varying visual cultures and is complicated in terms of classification. As we note elsewhere (see the section on simulacra in Chapter 6) cities have heterogeneous spaces where diverse cultural and historical buildings sit side by side.

These are all valid examples of what constitutes 'image' yet to focus solely on these modes of representation is to limit any discussion on or about 'image' as it excludes the potential for the image as a system of interpretation. It overlooks the importance of the image for the spectator in today's society where image *is* culture. The use of the word 'image' in this chapter has been referring to what is presented visually, that is questioning what it is about the image that forms part of a visual culture via any source or medium of media. The construction of a music artist's image such as Eminem, Britney Spears, Madonna, or on a group scale like Linkin Park or Atomic Kitten, contributes to the formation of an image that comes to represent a particular cultural group. These celebrities operate as synecdoches for hip-hop, pop culture and their 'image' is a creation formed to elicit investment of subjectivity from their fans. The image, seen working in this manner, is not restricted to the field of representation. Instead image has a more active role and place within culture, and has become a more dominating and driving force within culture than the written word and it is necessary to look at the implications of such a significant change. This form of image construction is two-fold. It acknowledges the economic value of the image as it produces money and is the equivalent of money at a merchandising level. In contrast, this construction is also the image to be looked at and desired. It is created to invite the gaze of the individual and the collective. In the overt style formation of music groups like those from the *Popstars* TV shows or Atomic Kitten, or individuals such as Kylie Minogue, Elvis or Madonna, this double working of the image is clearly apparent. However, with regards to the image of such groups as the Rolling Stones, the Beatles or INXS, it is suggested (as part of their image) that they 'style' themselves.

One aspect of the image and its operation in visual theory and in forming a visual culture is that the image is interdiscursive and relies on the spectator to become fully realized. The image is a component in a complex configuration of political, cultural and social discourses and ideologies formulating visual culture. When we, as spectators, rest our gaze on the image we are not simply viewing a flat, singular, secular piece of art (whether it be painting, a commercial, scene from a movie, buildings, photograph or a fashion show), instead we are incorporating ourselves into a chain of events – the process of creating culturally viable, sustainable and recognizable images. It is our part in reading and investing in the image as spectators that allows the image to grow with other images into a visual culture.

Barthes, in *The Fashion System* (1990), analyses fashion as a signification system, in written, real and photographic forms. His study highlighted how the image is created and endowed with cultural significance through the spectator's interpretation. This approach concentrates on the cultural operation of the image (in this case fashion) rather than focusing on what the image (fashion) *is*. It is the formation of the image – how it comes to possess meaning and how this meaning becomes understood, current and socially integrated within culture and specific cultural areas – that is to be considered even in something as visually simple as clothing. An example of how an image grows into a visual cultural process/narrative can be found in Vivienne Westwood's t-shirts[g] made at the height of punk. Wearing these confrontational t-shirts was seen as a punishable and criminal offence; some owners were told to take off their t-shirts in public by the police. Here Westwood used the fashion of t-shirts to exploit the potential and capacity of the image and its power within culture. The trend of punk, to rebel provocatively, was the propelling force behind the viability and social currency of the Westwood punk t-shirts. What was being expressed through the 't-shirt' was the agenda of punk – the rebellion of desire in youth, rebellion against establishmentarianism, and desire for an age of sexual liberation (both homosexuality and feminism).

The Westwood t-shirt in the 1970s drew on the inter-discursivity of the image to vocalize particular political agendas of a certain sub-cultural group. The body, used to support the t-shirt, was employed as a canvas to support a burgeoning sub-culture. Westwood viewed the world of fashion and models as a platform, not for *prêt-à-porter* collections (such as her fashion does in its post-punk epoch), but as a release for socially repressed sub-cultures such as punk. Now Vivienne Westwood's fashion designs and creations have shifted into high culture, where only the very rich and famous can afford to purchase and perhaps wear them. Her tone is still flamboyant but medically dispensed. It doesn't encourage or propel a political cultural movement, instead it reinforces the *haute couture* of fashion. There seems to be little force behind her collections except for the odd touch of feminism. Whilst before, her 1970s fashion helped give birth to the sub-culture of punk in Britain through image for political reasons, today her fashion sustains fashion as a branch of visual culture.

Barthes' work is influential on the recent disciplines of visual cultures and visual theory, especially for the spectator as it brings into focus the relationships between images and the spectator, between images and other images and all possible cultural interactions and positionalities. His work on the text has been a particularly influential force in cultural studies and areas of critical theory as it concerns itself with the reader's engagement with the text on a level interested more in the act of reading than the status of the text alone. Continuing with the fashion example, the brand Levi's jeans (and its product) provides a clear example of the interaction between image and spectator, both within a visual culture and beyond it. Originally a signifier for the working class in the 1880s, Levi's denim shifted its fabric across class and purpose. In the 1950s, with the likes of James Dean and Marlon Brando, jeans began to form an attitude and became an image worth investing in. Now the classic roots of Levi's have moved from representing the working class and masculinity to representing the affluence of the middle classes and are worn unisex. The first intentions for the use of Levi's as working gear are long lost and now issues of gender, class and what is deemed culturally fashionable dominate each representation and advertisement of the product. No longer do the advertisements carry the same wit and sense of rebellion as they once did, for Levi's has fulfilled its object. A culture born from 'image' has been created. To buy a pair of Levi's is to buy into something much larger on a cultural, and indeed a global, scale. Adorning the living body with a pair of Levi's jeans returns the body to the culture of cool that Levi's created in advertisements from the 1970s. In setting up this particular discourse for Levi's jeans, what resulted became more than simply buying a product. It was *Levi's* jeans that were the only jeans to have. The advertisements not only displayed and paraded a desirable and bankable persona; through the jeans they maintained a historical development that reflected one of the essential functions of Levi's jeans – which is that they stand the test of time both in fashion and in wear. Here we witness a cultural investment in fashion as culture and fashion as product.

This is crucial to any development or extension of visual cultures theory, as it enables the discipline to look at different forms of image-media and image-representation and, more specifically, regard this heterogeneity of image production within its genre as well as with other diverse institutions of thought outside what is directly produced for the visual.

The social order of the image: seeking pleasure

[T]he image – grasped immediately by an inner metalanguage, language itself – in actual fact has no denoted state, is immersed for its very social existence in at least an initial layer of connotation, that of the categories of language.

(Barthes 1977: 28)

We know that every language takes up a position with regard to things, that it connotes reality, if only in dividing it up; the connotations of the photograph would thus coincide, *grosso modo*, with the overall connotative planes of language.

(Barthes 1977: 29)

Such are the two ways of the Photograph. The choice is mine: to subject its spectacle to the civilised code of perfect illusions, or to confront in it the wakening of intractable reality.

(Barthes 1984: 119)

Like semiotics' sense of the sign, the image is not meaningful on its own. Barthes approaches the image systematically and his readings of images, whether they be cultural artifices or photographs, are interpreted via semiology as though it were a science. Tied into this Barthesian method is the concept of pleasure – both as a concept and a discourse. What is of interest in determining a social order of the image, and subsequently the place and importance of pleasure within, is how the image and the spectator, through a myriad of relations, construct and seek pleasure. The spectator's pleasures to be found in the image, in interacting with the image, recognizing the image and being recognized in return, are only some of the pleasures that Barthes examined. Only through an engagement with a set of recognized relations and code systems within culturally specific discourses, does the image become meaningful. It is through various positionalities produced by these cultural signifying systems that the image becomes a central thread in the social fabric. It is the social formation of the image within a cultural order, and the spectator's role in the creation of the image, in which we are interested.

Studium and punctum

In *Camera Lucida* Barthes works through the concept and signification of the photograph in culture, and how its combination of elements produces meaning in certain contexts, and how a message can exist *without* a code. For Barthes, the interaction and relationship between the spectator and the photographic image is a cultural one. What the spectator uses to interpret/read the image comes from a range of archived images received and produced by a specific socio-cultural discourse. In particular, Barthes reads from a French perspective and as a result, his comments on culture, the images produced by French culture or not, are always going to be read within a French frame for him. To work through the cultural effect and meaning of the photograph, Barthes appropriates the Latin terms *studium* and *punctum*. He uses these terms specifically for photography, but they have considerable potential for any discussion of the image. (They are also particularly relevant for any understanding of Barthes and his ideas on culture and the aesthetic.) For Barthes, *studium* is that aspect of the photograph, and arguably any image at all, that is culturally produced and received. No *studium* of an image can exist outside of an image, as this is the element through which the spectator forms meaning in their cultural field. Barthes states,

> It is by *studium* that I am interested in so many photographs, whether I
> receive them as political testimony or enjoy them as good historical
> sciences: for it is culturally (this connotation is present in *studium*) that I
> participate in the figures, the faces, the gestures, the settings, the actions.

> (Barthes 1984: 26)

In reading an image, we participate within this sense of the *studium*. We are culturally produced spectators and whether our interpretations of the image are submissive or aberrant – whether we read the image in its intended fashion or otherwise – we are reading it as representative of a cultural order and sensibility. For Barthes, this is the primary mode of interpreting the image or, in his case a photograph. The s*tudium* is a mirroring constituent that affirms the spectator's role in the discourse of the photograph, as well as their place in specific socio-cultural discourse when reading the photograph. In terms of applying or sketching out a social order of the image, the *studium* is the base from which all reading and interpretation is generated. It is via the *studium* that the image is contextualized. To further understand part of the *studium*'s function – why its concern is to culturally contextualize – is to understand what its relativity is in relation to pleasure.

The *studium* is the platform of recognition. In looking at the photograph *Afghan Girl*[h] by Steve McCurry (made famous as the cover of an issue of *National Geographic*) we recognize a number of elements. First, it is a photograph – we locate its typology of image. From this point any further comments stem from an engagement with *studium*, and these might be any interpretations from a judgement of what her face looks like, to the unifying colour that dramatizes the image (green of her eyes supported by green background), to her clothes, and even further towards events that are not in the photograph but are connotations of it. For example, 'in' the costume of the young girl is 'Afghanistan' – an indirect reference to Afghani culture and, subsequently, the young girl's socio-cultural and socio-economic status. This addresses another aspect of *studium,* which is recognition and receiving of the photographer's intentions. 'The *studium* is a kind of education (knowledge and civility, "politeness") which allows me to discover the *Operator*, to experience the intentions which establish and animate his practices, but to experience them "in reverse"' (Barthes 1984: 28) The spectator's comments on an image or photograph, whether they like or dislike it, and ideas about the photograph of the Afghan girl are produced along and within the discourse of the *studium*. We look at the photo and unconsciously mark it against the parameters of the *studium*. Not only are we working towards a recognition that exists on a simple level that is 'this is a photo of a girl' but also it is recognition of the photograph's implication in a wider cultural context, what it means in a Western phallocentric discourse, that we are recognizing.

We take pleasure in recognizing what is culturally recognizable and this is the *studium*'s objective – to become a platform for recognition of cultural images and codes. The spectator who views the image seeks and desires such recognition as it affirms their place in the social order of culture and in having it confirmed, gains pleasure through contextualizing an image in its relative cultural context. This includes the more obvious issue that we need cultural contexts in order to make sense of images (which can vary a great deal, from information to interpretation), to the more complex, such as formations of pleasure and desire, issues of hierarchy (such as class), the politics of gender, and so on. This flows on to Barthes' other term, that of the *punctum.*

The second Latin term that Barthes appropriates with respect to the photograph is *punctum*. Whereas the *studium* formed the cultural base of the photograph – both for the image itself and the spectator, the *punctum* is the element that shatters it – the disruptive element of the photograph. The relativity of Barthes' other agenda of pleasure comes into play here as the *punctum* operates similarly to *jouissance*[10] in that it is an indescribable, unfixable component of the image.

At the base of the social order of the image is how the spectator situates, or is situated by, his/her response to the image, and Barthes reads a number of photographs in this way. The *punctum* not only disrupts the *studium*'s cultural ordering of the photograph (or any image), but also the spectator's position. For Barthes, the *punctum* is individual to each spectator but its disturbing practice and effect is constant. It is the point where the spectator invests in the image, and begins to take part in the formation of the image's meaning. The *punctum* is essential to visual cultures as it marks the moment where the image moves from almost a backdrop in visual cultures to becoming the concentration of it. It does this through allowing, perhaps even provoking, the spectator to 're-view' the image. The *punctum* catches the gaze of the spectator and from this moment, works to subvert the codes that attempt to construct a whole, 'natural' composed image. Extending Barthes' *punctum* in this manner is moving beyond his initial classification, 'In order to perceive the *punctum*, no analysis would be of any use to me … it suffices that the image be large enough' (Barthes 1982: 42–3) but it takes up one of Barthes' other fundamental arguments – the birth of the reader – and encourages the spectator to use whatever *punctum* they find to reflect on and contribute to its disruptive questioning of the image and their relationship to it.

We have looked at Barthes' example of the Eiffel Tower in terms of narrative structure, and we can also use a similar example to discuss how such cultural signifiers are iconic. In *The Eiffel Tower and other Mythologies* (1979), Barthes discusses the iconic status of the image through the example of the Eiffel Tower. This ubiquitous image is symbiotic with any representation of France and/or Paris, and in itself is an apt example of how the image has come to usurp the written word. The Statue of Liberty is a comparable structure and its title 'The Statue of Liberty' does not offer the same impact or resonance as the icon itself. The image of the statue says America. It locates America and represents its preferred way of life, and in one image encapsulates all the other connotations of America that the reader/spectator has made, collated and referred to about the United States when interpreting additional relative icons. It has become more than a statue, for it has a visual and narrative presence throughout a great many visual texts, from cinema and television, advertising to fashion. It is an example of a visual image that always carries with it a powerful number of significations. In this sense The Statue of Liberty exceeds its own cultural and historical boundaries; it brings certain meanings to the other signs that are placed within a context to it.

In this sense, such use of a cultural icon enforces Barthes' point, that 'This pure – virtually empty – sign – is ineluctable, *because it means everything*. In order to negate the Eiffel Tower … you must … get up on it, and, so to speak, identify yourself with it' (Barthes 1993: 237). In 'meaning everything' – Barthes is highlighting how the image becomes inserted into, and a fundamental part of, the social fabric through a cultural investment into an image. Presenting images as systems of signs shifts the notion that an image is naturally perceived, and locates the image in a critical frame of discursive practice. The

Statue of Liberty does not actually represent America or all that is American, and yet it can appear to perform this function. The statue has become part of the spectator's socio-cultural fabric, thus creating the situation where to recognize this cultural icon is to recognize a constructed representation of the United States. The spectator's recognition is not invested or directed towards the lines that constitute the image of the Statue of Liberty, its creator, or indeed the artist or manufacturer representing the image of the statue, but towards the social order of the image via constructed codes. The social order of the image is recognized through the interaction between the image and other socio-cultural aspects.

Culture has always been interested in the image and its effect. From the earliest cave drawings to the Lumière brothers filming workers leaving the factory (in their train film) to more current practices of the image such as Damien Hirst's appropriation of everyday objects (like Panadol packets) into the status of contemporary art, to Martin Creed's[i] humorist Turner Prize-winning exhibit (in 2001) of an empty room where a light comes on and goes off at regular intervals, to Tracey Emin's submitting her own unmade bed[j] as an artistic piece. It is not so much the quality of image that captivates culture but its effect. Visual cultures, or a singular 'image', are not confined to the marbled halls of art galleries however. It is an unfixed, unstable concept that forms part of and produces part of culture and is omnipresent. The much-debated heroin-chic look of fashion models like Jodie Kidd and Kate Moss are images as performance, arresting the attention of the viewer through a projected or assumed effect. What is the result of an image's effect? What is the function and role of a spectator in terms of images in visual culture? These are fundamental questions to visual culture theory as they form the basis of shaping a spectating subject – that is, a conscious subject who critically engages with culturally produced images and plays a part in producing and circulating these images and their effect.

Notes

1 Bryson, Norman (2001) 'Semiology and Visual Interpretation' in Julia Thomas (ed.), *Reading Images*.

2 Semiotics is an interdisciplinary development that originally stems from linguistics and some fields of structuralism. In basic terms, semiotics is an analytical process that looks at the relationships between culture, society and meaning and their resulting creations. Barthes uses semiotics as a field of knowledge and applies it to other socio-cultural disciplines (see *Mythologies* (1973), London: Jonathan Cape) such as photography, film, art, sports and culture to highlight that it is to be used as a tool as much as a technique in the process of critical interpretation.

3 This is an example of how the image, as opposed to the literary text, is problematic in trying to separate the issue of representation from the network of relations that structure an image's signification.

4 See the chapter on power, where a more in-depth analysis of Foucault's work on Magritte can be found.

5 In much of Magritte's work the written language serves to test the relationship between the image and the word. We direct the reader to a particular piece by Magritte, *The Interpretation of Dreams* (1930).

6 Steve Irwin is a character, originally on Australian television, that hunts crocodiles and deals with other dangerous Australian creatures such as poisonous snakes and spiders. Largely the modes of his programmes are in a 'mockumentary' style and are filmed in outback Australia.

7 We refer the reader to Barthes' article 'Rhetoric of the Image', found in *Image-Music-Text*.

8 We refer the reader to the chapter 'The Death of the Author' found in *Image-Music-Text* – a fundamental entry into Barthes' opus and train of thought.

9 Compare this to the grain of the voice of Spike, which is overtly British, and in particular from London, designating another order of class.

10 This French term, *jouissance*, has been widely used and discussed in post-structuralism and psychoanalytic theory. In Barthes' mentioned text, Miller translates it as bliss, but to adhere to this translation is to miss the fundamental importance of the word that is (in part) excessive transgression and transgressive excess. Within this crude definition is the idea of sexual excess and transgression. *Jouissance* is purposely left untranslated so that the reader is not confused by the separate uses of pleasure and *jouissance*, and also to accustom the reader to important critical terminology.

a Yves Klein – *IKB 79*
 This image is not shown but the link below does provide some additional points about it.
 http://www.tate.org.uk/servlet/AText?id=8143&type=pit

b Nadar, *The Artist's Mother (or Wife)*
 http://www.pitt.edu/~schwerer/Nadar.html

c Magritte, *The Two Mysteries*
 Magritte, *The Treachery of Images* (referred to as *The Treason* of the pictures in the URL)
 http://www.ubmail.ubalt.edu/~pfitz/see/rm1/rm1gb_2_2.htm

 For various *tromp l'oeil*
 http://www.nga.gov/press/2002/exhibitions/deceptions/imagelist/images.htm

d McCubbin, *The Pioneer* (1904)
 http://www.ngv.vic.gov.au/collection/australian/painting/m/apa00043.html

e Duchamp, *L.H.O.O.Q.* (1920)
 http://www.boijmans.rotterdam.nl/onderw/thema/imitatio/imi6b.htm

f Freud's couch
 http://www.english.upenn.edu/~afilreis/freud-couch.html

g Vivenne Westwood's t-shirts
 http://www.mital-u.ch/PunkWave/index.html

h *Afghan Girl* – photograph by Steve McCurry
 http://www.nationalgeographic.com/ngm/100best/storyA_story.html
 http://magma.nationalgeographic.com/ngm/afghangirl/

i Martin Creed's work
 http://www.designboom.com/portrait/creed.html

j Tracey Emin, *My Bed*
 http://www.sussex.ac.uk/Units/arthist/sharp/issues/0002/pPDF/pTraceyEminMyBed.pdf

Chapter Six

INVISIBILITY AND ☐
HALLUCINATION

The state of the image in the postmodern world

Is this a dagger which I see before me, The handle towards my hand? Come,
let me clutch thee – I have thee not and yet I see thee still!

(Shakespeare, *Macbeth*)

Unlike the other chapters, here we will be looking at a range of different theories. One of
the most striking aspects of all the theorists in this chapter is just how visually orientated
their style is. This does not just include the metaphors and examples they employ, but also
the very substance of what they are attempting to do. Each of them works with the visual
in order to explain and explicate ideas, concepts and dilemmas drawn from a wide range
of disciplines, including philosophy, psychoanalysis, social theory, cultural praxis, media
studies and the sciences. Because we are concerned with some key theorists here, each
having produced a great many works, there is a need to keep things focused. What we lose
in coverage we should make up for by providing a more in-depth analysis of a particular
theme (and one that has resonance across a number of fields, including the works of the
theorists at hand).

The common link in this chapter will be how we might approach the issues and idea of
the visual that is not there, or has been problematized in terms of its status and existence.
This is the visual in terms of surfaces, hallucinations and simulacra. Although this
questionable status of the visual has a postmodernist feel about it, in fact it is one of the
oldest attributes of the relationship between image and spectator. For what often marks the
visible is indeed its absences, its shadows and its simulations. A key part of this is
authenticity; and every generation, every cultural and historical era, seems to have had
versions of this in terms of the image. How a cultural moment defines itself in terms of the
authenticity of the image determines so much of that culture's identity. As we have seen,
and will further observe in this section, from the end of the nineteenth century there has
been a sort of unauthentification of the image.

There is a certain irony to this, for with the refinement of scientific instruments that
allowed for images of previously unseen objects (from the minute particles seen through an
electron microscope to the galaxies revealed by the Hubble telescope) it would seem logical

that the image would become more authentic and certain during this period. Even with the mass of personal video cameras that have allowed multiple versions of news events (such as the Twin Towers disaster of September 11) to be captured, it would seem that in recent times there is a profusion of authentic (and authenticated) images within our culture. And yet, in conjunction with such visuals, we also see a questioning of the image and its authenticity through a series of complex theories and arguments, and, significantly, within the visual texts themselves. This is part of the agenda for the ensuing discussion.

This idea of authentification is necessarily complex, for it contains within it not just the status of the image (whether it is considered 'real' or 'false', whether it is seen as the original or a copy, and so on) but also our relationship to the image as spectators. Furthermore, there is a sort of cultural contextualizing involved – of how a culture orders its perspective on the authentic and inauthentic image, of how certain images become privileged as more authentic than others, and so on. This is a two-way process: on the one hand there is a cultural ordering to position images in this manner; and on the other there is a set of processes coming from the images themselves that determines how spectators relate to such positionings. This is perhaps nowhere more apparent than in relationships of images of faith and religious belief. To the devotee these images are more than representational for they carry in themselves an element of what they portray. Similarly, flag burning is an attack on a culture's authenticity as well as an assault on a visual metaphor. In the devotional image and the powerfully ideological one (such as a flag) what is ultimately being contested is this relationship of spectator to authenticity.

To investigate this, and related ideas, further we have divided this chapter into three sections. These are necessarily brief, and the reader is encouraged to make links between the ideas, even if the theorists themselves are not always working to the same level of accord. Our aim is to show how various ways of thinking can be utilized to examine this process of the image as a problematized presence. The first part will look at an idea from the philosopher and the psychoanalyst, Deleuze and Guattari. Their 'invention' of the rhizome is partly a strategy to rethink some fundamental ideas, as well as a method of analysis in itself. We will be interested in this in terms of the visual and the surface. The second section looks at the philosopher and cultural theorist Baudrillard and some of the key points on his notion of simulacra. We are particularly interested in how his notion can be developed to refigure the real of the image. To this end we have coined the term hyper-image. The third and final section will look at a range of ideas based on the relationship of the image and invisibility.

The image as rhizome

Hallucination is to the eye what truth is to the image. By this we mean that there is a constant struggle between the subject of the gaze (that is, when we are most defined by our relationship to the image) and the veracity of the image. This struggle is generated in many different ways, for many different effects. One example would be the resistance to what is being seen – the visual disbelief of what is unfolding before our eyes. The images of the destruction of the Twin Towers were so often described as unbelievable and so much like something out of a disaster film; the concentration camps of the Holocaust were described with incredulity – as if something this horrific could not exist. These examples of excessive witnessing, where the image confronts the spectator's very subjectivity and operates at a level of seeming disbelief, are extreme versions of what in fact takes place every day. It is no coincidence that the examples that immediately spring to mind tend to be those that are the most shocking, but the same could be argued for the most beautiful of images as well. Part of what these excessive witnessings involve is a type of self-reflexivity, where the spectator is positioned in an inescapable relationship to what is being seen, and yet also tries to resist its authenticity.

In the most simplistic of terms, we categorize images into the real and the unreal (the tree outside the window as distinct from the spaceships in a science fiction film), and have little difficulty making such differences. (It is noteworthy that the inability to do so defines a certain type of madness – note the slippage towards madness in Macbeth when he sees/imagines the dagger, as referred to at the opening of this chapter.) Yet the almost continual blurring of such a simple binarism is an essential part of our pleasures, desires and sense-making processes. A key element in any visual representation – from an advertisement to a painting, a film to a photograph – is the interplay between what we see and how it relates to us. Part of this pleasure and knowledge production is the visual's capacity to blur the real and unreal for us. A far more common example, and one less confronting than the examples of disaster footage and horrific prison camps, is the experience of looking at photographs of one's self but having a sense of disbelief about the self. Everyone experiences the feeling that some photographs look more like them than others; we will often hear the expression 'that doesn't look like me'. This implies that we have a sense of an image of ourselves that is quite specific – and yet why does a photograph that is actually of us deny that status? How is it that we can acknowledge that this is a photograph of ourself and yet say it doesn't look like us? Even if we separate out all the tricks of distortion, poor lighting, moments of odd facial expression, badly taken photographs, ravages of time, and so on, there are still those images that we say do not look like us, that seem to show a different sort of person. This is like Freud's famous story of how he was on a train and looked up to see a grumpy old man staring at him, only to realize that he had caught a glimpse of himself, quite unexpectedly, in a mirror. Part of this is that the image generates a sort of disbelief, the hallucinogenic effect, which brings into question its own truth as a representation.

This essential relationship, of the image's relationship to truth, is that it always contains an element of disbelief. What changes in cultural and historical contexts are the degrees of this belief, these acts of faith and trust in the image, and the shaping of the spectator's positioning in terms of the image. If what we are asserting is true, and that the past 100 years or so have seen a strengthening of the mistrust of the authentic and a shifting away from the idea of the primacy of originals, then it can be said that the visual culture of today is premised on the copy and the inauthentic.[1] It is important to recognize that this is not a negativity, and that what we are describing here is somehow a collapse of the (truth of the) image. However, it cannot be denied that one of the essential aspects of critical theory – from psychoanalysis to feminism, from semiotics to deconstruction – has been its challenge to the image. And it is in this that we witness a resolution to the irony of more precise documentation of the image (through science) and a proliferation of the image as confirmation of events. For what these theories have allowed is not the destruction of the image (and its authenticity) but rather a comprehensive set of theories that explore how the image operates within every facet of human activity.

To progress further with this interpretation let us take up some specific ideas, commencing with one that has a far more literary origin than a visual one – that of Deleuze and Guattari's idea of the rhizome. For a source so literary, the metaphor of the rhizome is strikingly visual.[2] The rhizome, we recall, is a plant with a root system that grows beneath and parallel to the ground. It sends up shoots at periodic intervals, as with various sorts of grasses. Thus the rhizome structure is one of surfaces and interconnected root systems; it is multiplicity rather than unary. It creeps along as a surface system rather than, say, with a tree, having roots that extend with depth. Deleuze and Guattari articulate a number of features of the rhizome as they develop it as a way of thinking through some of the complex issues of thought and analysis. Their interest is in exploring different ways of thinking and problematizing analysis itself. They are, after all, a philosopher and psychoanalyst with a deep political commitment. Their projects explore many cultural processes, but perhaps the one consistent theme is that of subjectivity. From *Anti-Oedipus: Capitalism and Schizophrenia*, with its socio-political analysis of desire, through to Guattari's final work *Chaosmosis: An Ethico-Aesthetic Paradigm*, subjectivity has always been the driving force. What locates these works within a sense of an ongoing project is rethinking subjectivity outside of the dominant models and ideas. The works of Deleuze and Guattari offer a constant state of challenge to the ways in which we are located within the social order. In this sense the idea of the rhizome is orientated towards how we might reposition the individual in terms of the group, as well as offering strategies to resist what Foucault once called the fascist way of life.[3] We can adapt what they are doing to think differently about the image, to look for points of resistance in looking. At the same time we can witness the ways in which the image features in some of their works.

CONNECTION

'Any point on a rhizome can be connected with any other, and must be. This is very different from a tree or root, which fixes a point and thus an order' (Deleuze and Guattari 1983: 11). Thus the rhizome opens up connections, for its very existence depends on them. In a way we can read this as a type of intertextuality, with one occurrence/text immediately demanding reference to another. However, if we are to read it in this way we must be careful not to underestimate the primacy of such connections. A rhizomic connection is essential, not just an adjunct; within such an organization the spectator cannot observe the image without making various connections. The image cannot even make sense without such connections, and we can even go so far as to say that it would fail to exist.

What is perhaps of even greater significance, however, is that these connections are not just to other images. Instead the rhizomic feature of connections extends across a vast array of subjects, and is in a constant state of production: 'A rhizome *never ceases* to connect semiotic chains, organizations of power, and events in the arts, sciences, and social struggles' (Deleuze and Guattari 1983: 12, emphasis added). Let us discount two examples of connection as not being truly rhizomic in nature. The first is when an image is employed for a different function than it is normally seen to perform. In 2002, for example, environmental scientists used paintings of the canals in Venice over hundreds of years old to monitor the rising water levels. This became a newsworthy item because the artworks were connected to a scientific investigation (and so multiple connections, from Venice's buildings, to their representation in painting, to science, to the mass media). The problem with seeing this in terms of a Deleuzian/Guattarian rhizome is that there is still a force within all this that attempts to preserve the origins of the image. The paintings are still seen as paintings, but are being 'translated' for a different function. However, the intervention of the mass media is closer to a different level of connection, because it is an intervention on a different sort of level. We shall return to this example later to see how it can be used more within the sense of the rhizome.

The second sort of example we wish to exclude is when a connection is made with a sort of direct intentionality. When Picasso 'repaints' Velázquez's *Las Meninas*[a] we are not really in the presence of a rhizome because the connection tends to be quite linear and unary. We recognize the reference and the adaptation, and we acknowledge the processes of connecting different artistic worlds, and we even recognize the postmodernist reflexivity of Picasso's style. However, these are so strong that other connections tend to be repressed, and we end up seeing these connections beyond all else.

Whilst these two examples have qualities of the rhizome because they exist so much within a sense of connections, we really need to look elsewhere to see the sorts of qualities that Deleuze and Guattari are devising in the term. In order to understand this we need to turn to the second quality they list.

HETEROGENEITY

The rhizome doesn't simply connect things, it forcibly makes connections with a vast array of disciplines. In doing so it produces an analytic moment, where the qualities of one system become enmeshed and infused with other systems. Or, to put it another way, the forces of preservation and homogeneity are broken down through the connections. This produces heterogeneity within the internal structures. Deleuze and Guattari give the example of language, arguing that a rhizome approach sees language as a diverse system, challenging the idea of a centralized and stable language: 'A method of the rhizome type … can only analyze language by de-centering it onto other dimensions and into other registers' (Deleuze and Guattari 1983: 13). So for them it is not just a matter of looking at the diversity of language, but the analysis itself only becomes possible by bringing such aspects to the fore.

This may become clearer if we try some specific visual examples. City spaces are great examples of these aspects of connection and heterogeneity because they are built up over time and through various cultural forces. So the initial connections we tend to make regarding the functionality and architecture of buildings give way to a much wider range of connections when seen as a rhizome. This in turn introduces a much stronger sense of heterogeneity into the visual spaces. Look, for example, at the city spaces of some modern cities – Boston, London and Sydney are all good examples.[4] Each has a business district, a shopping area, public parks and gardens – all the elements that constitute 'cityness'. However, the more interesting rhizomes of space in these cities are those that have abutments and layering that works at an extraordinarily visual level. The Chinatown/Soho area of London, the Chinatown/financial area of Boston, and the King's Cross/Rushcutter's Bay area of Sydney contain connections that produce a great many heterogeneous influences and effects. There is the excess of 'ethnic' signifiers (in these examples non-Western), the streets of sex shops, and the movement back into Western offices and shops or affluent suburbs. The rhizome of these city spaces is the absolute diversity of origins, functions and identities. To walk through these spaces (and often it can take no more than ten or fifteen minutes) is to pass through aspects that have no real connection except that they are designated as liminal, non-centralized and edgy by the dominant order. Ethnicity and sexuality define the spaces within themselves, but it is the wandering of the spectator that produces the rhizome.

What this example demonstrates is that the rhizome of something like a city space allows different sorts of connections to be revealed. The pornography shops and the Chinese and Vietnamese restaurants they sit beside are defined as Other by the censoring city, but their connection to each other (through exclusion) and to the dominant city (through patronage and popularity) produces the heterogeneity of the modern city itself. By approaching this as a rhizome we observe Deleuze and Guattari's point regarding the de-centring process into 'other dimensions and into other registers'. The rhizome acknowledges the city as a visually heterogeneous space and breaks down the idea of a centre. This brings us to the third point, that of multiplicity.

MULTIPLICITY

Two key aspects of the rhizome in terms of multiplicity are that 'multiplicities are rhizomatic, and expose arborescent pseudo-multiplicities', and that 'there are no points or positions in a rhizome, as one finds in a structure, tree or root. There are only lines' (Deleuze and Guattari 1983: 14, 15). Of course the recurring image in these points is the metaphor of the tree opposed to the rhizome, which is the unary as distinct from the multiple. As with heterogeneity, what distinguishes multiplicity in the rhizome is that it is an essential feature of the analysis – it cannot be used unless these aspects are integrated into the analysis. In turn, these qualities are introduced into the point of what is being analysed. For our concerns here this means that the image is a multiplicity of lines, rather than a single defining point. It is this snaking out, these on-going lines of connection, that defines the analytic (and productive) aspects of the rhizome.

There are many ways we can utilize such an idea in the analysis of the visual. As with the city spaces we noted a moment ago, what constitutes, enables and forms such spaces are these connections. Certainly it is possible to stand in the centre of Chinatown and observe the images of a specific ethnic group, but in a city such as London there are always lines (Londoners themselves, the English buildings on the horizon, the manhole covers on the sewerage, the prices in pounds sterling) that take this to a multiplicity rather than a point of centre. The lines of flight in such a scene push the connections, produce the multiplicities, so that the spectator is always taken elsewhere. The visual is particularly good at this sort of thing, but it is not something that comes easily to the image. This is because we are taught to read the image as a centring moment, or contained within the frame (be it a literal frame, such as around a painting, or that myriad of signifiers that operate as frames – from the street borders around a city space to the skin of the body). The rhizomic image always contests unification.

A-SIGNIFYING RUPTURE

Deleuze and Guattari actually use an image as an example of this attribute of the rhizome. Basically they are dealing with the idea that there cannot be a stabilized meaning within the rhizome, or even a dominant and on-going sense to it. This is because the rhizome can be broken at any point and yet still continues on, making its lines of connection in other ways. Within the rhizome, then, signification is more problematical, with meanings continually being renegotiated and devised. Here is the example given by Deleuze and Guattari:

> The orchid is deterritorialized by forming an image, an exact tracing (*calque*) of the wasp; but the wasp reterritorialized, however, by becoming part of the orchid's reproductive apparatus, but it reterritorializes the orchid by transporting its pollen. The wasp and the orchid thus make a rhizome, insofar as they are heterogeneous.
>
> (Deleuze and Guattari 1983: 19)[5]

The example of the orchid impersonating (that is, creating an image) of the wasp in order to make itself appear as something different, and then the wasp making itself appear more like the orchid, is rhizomic because the meaning of the image is constantly being referred to as a different signifying practice. This allows Deleuze and Guattari to develop one of their most important ideas – that of 'becoming'. Through the operation of the rhizome the orchid becomes a wasp, and the wasp becomes an orchid. As we saw before, the scientists used the paintings of Venice so that they became instruments of science, and in a way we have a becoming-art of science.

The key aspect here of note is that this 'becoming' process that the rhizome allows (indeed requires) works on the level of signification. In other words this is a direct engagement with the issues of meaning and understanding. Recalling that for Deleuze and Guattari a primary concern must always be with the formations of subjectivity, what resonance does this have for the spectator? What we would argue here is that when we engage in the image (that is, when the image becomes of concern, interest, desire, pain, and so on), we are in a state of becoming-spectator. Just as the wasp and orchid shift the levels of signifying for each other, so, too, do the spectator and the image. The subject is deterritorialized (that is, positioned outside of its normal boundaries) by the image, and the image is deterritorialized by the spectator, as each enters into a relationship of meaning. To look at the face of a loved one – a partner, a child – is quite different from looking at the face of a stranger. The lines of connection for the loved one (those rich emotions of love and care, of emotional histories, of memories) compared to the stranger is a-signifying because they push far beyond the image. This is part of the reason that Deleuze and Guattari specify this as an 'a-signifying rupture', for determining meaning gives way to the impossibility of fixing meaning.

An important part of these processes is that the rhizome brings together two (or possibly more) quite distinct elements. It is the heterogeneity of the two elements (wasp and orchid) that produces the rhizome – that is, a fresh line of difference in the pattern of signification. It is, in this sense, a rupturing process. Our example of the face works differently, yet in a similar fashion. What is it, for example, when someone falls in love with the face of a film star? The merging of the stranger with the loved one produces something that is not taken as the same type of response to either the countless productions of star images, or the specific set of images of the loved ones. We cannot think that someone can be in love with the image on the screen, and yet clearly this is often the way it is described. The rupturing effect is that the sense of intimacy is transposed onto the total stranger. Perhaps this is the rhizomic effect of when we see a photograph of ourselves but see a stranger instead of the familiar. Guattari, in *Molecular Revolution: Psychiatry and Politics*, asks the following question: 'What is it that is operating in what one sees as the *features* of a face, a landscape, a body? How do we account for the mystery of a particular look, a thing, a street, a memory? What is actually there to see seems to be concealing something else' (Guattari 1984: 154). This is the process of memory as it confirms or denies what is being seen at the time. What we think we should be seeing is a measure from memory that may or may not match what is before our eyes. The rhizome of the image is an investigation of such disturbances. Surrealist paintings work in a similar way to create ruptures of meaning. There is something altogether rhizomic in a Magritte or Dali painting as they collapse lines of connection from quite different sources.[6]

We can approach this from a different visual example. Memory in films can be used to confirm or disturb what the characters and spectator expect to see. In *Memento* (Nolan 2000) memory is presented as an untrustworthy and falsifying process; the mental processes of remembering are replaced by the corporeal messages (as Leonard Shelby writes to himself notes that become cryptic when they are re-read). Similarly, in *Mulholland Drive* (Lynch 2001) memory is continually asserted to problematize the present and make planning the future almost impossible. The mystery exists because Rita cannot remember her past, and together the two women try to construct what becomes a joint memory. We see the same sort of process (and narrative development) in Jacques Rivette's *Celine and Julie Go Boating* (1974) – the mystery of a conjoined narrative where two women must share enigmatic memories. In all three films memory becomes the rhizome as it refuses to grow roots and instead continually extends in multiple directions. Compare this to Hitchcock's *Spellbound* (1945), which is much less rhizomic as it traces and directs the memories of John Ballantine so that eventually they become more sensible and explanatory. Tracings such as these, and their differences, lead us into the final points on the rhizome.

CARTOGRAPHY AND DECALCOMANIA

Much of the way in which Deleuze and Guattari define the rhizome is through contrast; it is defined as much by what it is not, what functions it resists and refuses to perform, as by what it is. In this sense they describe the rhizome against the idea of copy and tracing, and much more like the map. Once more we can note just how strikingly visual this aspect of the rhizome is, drawing on lines and contours, shapes and copies, to explain processes of analysis. Their argument draws on the idea of types of thinking that replicate and copy. For them this is the replication and preservation of ideas across time and culture. So a process of tracing commences with something – an idea or system of thought, for example – already present and then follows this process. A rhizome, on the other hand, does not trace, rather it maps. The rhizome as map is far more inventive and experimental: 'The map is open, connectable in all its dimensions, and capable of being dismantled; it is reversible and susceptible to constant modification … . Perhaps one of the most important characteristics of the rhizome is that it always has multiple entrances' (Deleuze and Guattari 1983: 26).[7]

It is interesting to note that the examples that Deleuze and Guattari continually refer to in discussing this issue of the map are the subjects of psychoanalysis – specifically the children in analysis (Freud's Little Hans and Melanie Klein's Little Richard). It is not so important for us to know these case studies (although they are readily available: see Freud's case study of Little Hans and Klein's *Narrative of a Child Analysis*), for the real point is that these children are seen as map-makers (and therefore producing rhizomes) whilst psychoanalysis is in a constant state of tracing their actions and deeds back onto something (the family, photographs, sketches drawn by the child). (Deleuze and Guattari argue that the map is performance whilst the trace is linked to competence.) What we can take from this is the sense that the rhizome may seem like madness, but it really has its own internal logic and sense-making forms.

Decalcomania is the process of transferring images via tracing. It is, then, the opposite of cartography in this schema. Magritte has a painting, called *Décalcomanie*[b] (1966), which features his famous bowler-hatted man. The painting shows a back view of the man looking out onto a beach scene with white clouds and blue skies. Beside him is a brown curtain that has a cut-out version of the figure, the space of the man renders visible the same beach scene. It is an image full of those wonderful Magritte moments, of play and illusion, of making us think about how we occupy space, of the force of the visible, the contrasts between nature and culture, and the problematized role of humanity in such an order. All of these aspects (and there are so many more) operate in the ways in which Deleuze and Guattari describe the map of the rhizome – only Magritte has managed to construct a rhizome out of the established acts of tracing!

This painting by Magritte is significant in another way here. Deleuze and Guattari are fully aware of the traps of binarism. After all, they are suggesting a method of thinking that purposefully operates through multiplicities rather than binary divides. They acknowledge that it would go against their whole system if cartography were to be seen as the mirror opposite of tracing. They even admit that mapping can appear to be a form of tracing at times. Magritte's painting works in much the same way as Deleuze and Guattari would like us to think about the rhizome as map. It is inventive and dispersing rather than explaining and fixing. It provokes an originality that makes us question the whole visual process, and in doing so challenges much more than art. The rhizome, like another of their key ideas, nomadism, is designed to cause wandering ideas rather than resolutions. The style of all this can be disconcerting, but when it works there is something quite liberating about the whole thing. To follow this up some more we can turn to another writer who can be just as abstract and expansive: Baudrillard.

Simulacra

One of Baudrillard's key ideas is that of simulacra, and it is one that informs a great deal of his writing. Baudrillard investigates the relationship between the real and the copy, between the authentic and the false. In doing so he challenges one of the basic premises of Western thought – that there is an original (an *eidos*) that is distinct from the copy. Baudrillard goes against the line developed by Plato, arguing instead that everything is a copy of a copy, and that we exist in a world of simulation and simulacra.[8] What Deleuze and Guattari describe as the surface structure of the rhizome can be compared to Baudrillard's idea of imitation. Although we must be wary of such a comparison, for eventually there are distinctions to be made, not the least is that, as we noted above, the rhizome and nomadism are seen as a type of creative strategy to thinking anew, while Baudrillard is attempting to explicate the nature of simulacra as it has come to be formed in our contemporary social order.

With this precaution in mind let us turn to a specific example of the simulacra as Baudrillard figures it. Around a month after the United Nations Security Council (in 1991) agreed to a war against Iraq, Baudrillard published an essay entitled 'The Gulf War Will Not Take Place'; he then wrote two more pieces – 'The Gulf War: Is It Really Taking Place?' and 'The Gulf War Did Not Take Place'.[9] They are, of course, provocative titles because something called the Gulf War did obviously take place at this time. Baudrillard's argument rests in part on his theorizing of the simulacra and the role of the mass media. The Gulf War was a highly televised event – receiving the most coverage in the mass media of any war, perhaps of any conflict to date. The later conflict in Afghanistan could be said to equal that amount of coverage, and certainly worked in a similar style. The world was presented with intricate maps of once unheard-of places (for the majority of the West at least), extensive meteorological information about climate changes and seasonal extremes, armament details, population figures, and so on. It is this sort of information overload that contributes to Baudrillard's reading of the negation of a war as such. In both the Gulf War and the conflict in Afghanistan the images of war were remarkable in their detachment from humanity. We experienced visuals like never before (cameras on bombs took the spectator into the heart of the destruction) and yet it seemed as if no one was actually dying because the bodies of war were absent from the screens. In this sense it was a simulacra, an event too precisely conducted to seem real. As a representation, the Iraq and Afghanistan conflicts did not fit into what people had been used to. The Vietnam War was famous for having been taken into people's living rooms; these later wars took the next step and became programmed events.

There is another level to these simulacra, but it is equally dependent on the images from the mass media. For Baudrillard it is the next phase of war, a playing-out of a particular type of ideology. As he puts it:

> The real warmongers are those who live on the veracity of this war, while the war itself wreaks havoc at another level of trickery, hyperreality, simulacra, and by the entire mental strategy of deterrence which is played out in the facts and in the images, in the anticipation of the real by the virtual, of the event by virtual time, and in the inexorable confusion of the two.
>
> (Baudrillard 1995: 67)

The point here is that, yes, a war did take place in the Gulf, and countless people died in that conflict; but there is further conflict being played out at another level of reality. In one way this is comparable to what we discussed in the Foucault chapter – it is a complex interplay of the image and power with the spectator being at once instructed and potentially resisting the readings. It is this confusion of the two that makes this a hyperreal event.

Hyperreality is, for Baudrillard, something more real than the real. It is a quality that has come to exemplify the contemporary world, and it works particularly effectively in the domain of the visual. As Baudrillard puts it: '... the real is hyperrealised. Neither realised, nor idealised: but hyperrealised. The hyperreal is the abolition of the real not by violent destruction, but by its assumption, elevation to the strength of the model' (Baudrillard 1983: 84). The film *The Matrix* did get it right in this regard. The computer-generated world that Neo must expose is the hyperreal; and it did destroy the real through its assumption. And this is the point about the coverage of the Gulf War. It is not simply the treatment of it by the mass media, but the hyperreal ideologies that were generated out of the conflict. It is worth noting that this may well be exemplified by the recent conflicts, but they are by no means unique.

Hyperreality would seem to develop a type of acute and potent force with emerging technologies. It is the new media (and here we would include cinema) that has allowed this to take place. Interestingly Walter Benjamin's essay 'The Work of Art in the Age of Mechanical Reproduction', written in the early part of the twentieth century, anticipates precisely this point. He closes the essay with the following point:

> Thus, for contemporary man the representation of reality by the film is incomparably more significant than that of the painter, since it offers, precisely because of the through going permeation of reality with mechanical equipment, an aspect of reality which is free of all equipment. And that is what one is entitled to ask from a work of art.
>
> (Benjamin 1996: 135)

The hyperreality of cinema (both literally the extraordinary effects that make the impossible seem real, as well as the sorts of things that Benjamin is talking about here) is now joined by the internet, theme parks, interactive museum exhibits, the video screens in Times Square and at sporting arenas, and television.

The other key aspect to Baudrillard's notion of hyperreality is his working-out of simulation. Of course this is also part of the whole issue of simulacra, but the emphasis is on a type of excess. Just as hyperreality is more real than the real, so simulation is a level of excessive information that looks to be meaningful, but rather has a questionable status in this regard. Baudrillard positions this within a range of aspects: 'They have become more social than the social (the masses), fatter than fat (obesity), more violent than the violent (terror), more sexual than sex (porn), more real than the real (simulation), more beautiful than the beautiful (fashion)' (Baudrillard 1988: 83). The visual of course forms a key aspect within such processes, and in determining the visual culture of a moment so much of this simulation/information becomes embedded in the currency of the image. It is this exchange value of images that comes to determine a cultural identity (and crisis) both for a cultural order in itself and for others. How the social, violence, sexuality, sense of beauty, and the body are rendered as images is also how the social order constructs exchange processes (including the gift). Such images in turn become hyper-images because they are not just images of what they represent, but also of a cultural perspective. At the beginning of the twenty-first century, for example, the hyper-image of violence has become terrorism, in the 1980s and 1990s the hyper-image of the body became the excesses of thinness for women and muscularity for men.

We designate these as hyper-images, in part because they operate (as mentioned above) through a sort of 'more image than image' relationship to what they represent. This means that they do not simply present a more extreme version of the thing being represented, these hyper-images actually shift the signification of the thing within its social order. The hyper-image, almost ironically, can become the defining image for that which it comes to represent because it is such an extreme version. This happens in a myriad of different ways, and for differing reasons. The *Mona Lisa*^c is a hyper-image of 'art' because it is impossible to look at it now other than as a famous painting. Whatever currency it had, whatever aesthetic exchange value was attached to it once, has given way to an excessive image of art. Similarly, with the development of the star system in Hollywood, celebrity has made actors' faces and bodies hyper-images. It is almost impossible to look at a photograph of Humphrey Bogart and not hear his distinctive voice and think of something like *Casablanca*; or see an image of Brigitte Bardot and recognize a version of French sexuality. What we do not see, however, are the people themselves.

All of this ties into another of the key aspects of these hyper-images. That is, that they all rely, at some level, on absence. The hyper-image of violence as terrorism relies on an unending provocation of possible terrorist acts, most (if not all) of which do not take place. However, the function of the image of terrorism, for the terrorist organization, for the state it opposes, and for the general population, is this sense of possibility. The more effective this becomes, the more the images of terrorism become hyperreal. Similarly, the hyper-image of both masculine and feminine bodies could never actually be articulated through a human body – it is a carefully staged process of photograph, lighting, air-brush touch-ups, impossible lifestyles and diets, and so on. As a final example, think of the ways in which religious iconography operates as a hyper-image. The acts of faith bestowed on them work through the absence of the thing represented. Furthermore, the greater the extremes of such image the stronger the demand to faith. Yet such demands make the representations hyper-images. Buildings such as the Duomo in Florence or Notre Dame in Paris have become hyper-images of places of worship, as well as buildings themselves. Gaudi recognized this architectural force and allowed his designs to declare themselves as much images as buildings.

Another interesting aspect of hyper-images is that they will often try to deny this status, and will include 'claims' that they are presenting the normal. This process of naturalization is important to the hyper-image in its attempts to work within the cultural order of things. In the era of the supermodel, women's bodies had to seem both real and hyper-real. When Elle McPherson was designated 'The Body' it was equally important that her corporeality was seen as human, as well as allowing for this sense of the hyper-image. Similarly, even with the thousands of tourists pressing through the doors of a famous cathedral there is always an attempt to make it seem a place of worship.

Let us recap at this point on some of the key aspects of the image and simulation in terms of the hyper-image. The following checklist is by no means complete, but it will give us a reasonable sense of what has gone before.

- Hyper-images are produced through a variety of different processes (culturally, ideologically, historically, textually), some becoming invested with this status immediately, others gaining it over time.
- They are images that become 'translated' into hyper-images through these different processes. For example, a painting can be translated into 'art' and then into a hyper-image through history, the status of the artist, or the ideological processes that come to surround the subject matter. Or, to take another example, the body is translated into the supermodel/actor/celebrity by being located in a particular type of medium, violence into terrorism through political agendas, a church into a hyper-image of faith through the tourist trade, and so on.
- The hyper-image relies on absences to construct and retain part of its power. Through these absences it seduces the spectator into a contributory role. In other words, the hyper-image self-perpetuates by convincing the spectator of its status.
- The hyper-image alters the exchange value of the image. Once an image gains this status its 'value' alters and, even more importantly, it alters the exchange and commodification values within that cultural order. The hyper-image of the body is more corporeal – which could mean more beautiful, more powerful, even more abject (in a slasher film, for example) – and therefore shifts the value system of bodies within that cultural moment.
- The hyper-image will always attempt to retain part of its original significance (the *Mona Lisa* has a force which attempts to locate it back into the domain of painting; the supermodel/actor/celebrity attempts to become a person again), and yet the drive of the simulation always prevents this. Once figured as a hyper-image it is almost impossible to revert. Such a reversal does take place, of course, but the image will always retain some aspects of its excess. Painters, for example, go in and out of fashion (Crivelli was immensely popular for late Victorian England, but has less of a status within the current cultural moment) but for certain groups that status of the hyper will remain.
- The hyper-image occupies a dual space – both a part of and apart from the cultural order. It has the capacity to define a cultural moment, and yet can also be seen to stand out from all the other images generated by that culture.
- The hyper-image can become an archetype so that it becomes more essential than what it represents. In this sense it is tied to an ideological process, often working as a defining image (potentially either negatively or positively) – the small moustache underneath the nose has become a hyper-image of Hitler and as such has changed the cultural value of such a facial adornment.
- Finally, the hyper-image has in itself no intrinsic qualities. Anything has the potential to be translated into such a thing. It is dependent solely on external forces and processes. Thus the hyper-image is not valued in itself, but for what it has become.

Invisibility and the outcast of the image

The final section of this chapter is not centred on any one theorist; rather it is driven and informed by a matrix of ideas that might at one level be called postmodernist, and at another something like the posthuman. Perhaps we will discover that ultimately they are the same thing, but even with differences we can be certain that the two will often meet, and each always inform the other in some manner. There is always a danger in attempting to locate a wide range of ideas and theoretical perspectives within a single frame, and one should be nervous about any line that melds such complexities together. The defence here is as it has been throughout the book – that we are primarily concerned with the formation and operation of visual cultures and the theoretical resonances involved. This is why we close this section, and the book, with a consideration of invisibility.

Invisibility is not the antithesis of the visual, and as we noted above, visibility (that is, the formation of a culture through its images) depends extensively on what is not seen. This is more complex than at first seems to be the case, and to work through some of these ideas we will take up a number of issues that reflect exactly the complexity involved. Part of the focus is the political agenda – of the ways in which some things are made visible and others invisible. The idea that we are pursuing is that cultures do not only make some things more visible, but they necessarily make others invisible. Furthermore, the condition of invisibility operates not simply as a negation of these things, but as a requirement to their existence. Let us take this in stages, and through some examples show the invisibility of visual culture.

INVISIBLE GENDERS

The most visible presence in Hollywood cinema is white males. Any variation on this usually requires, or at least offers up, some form of qualifying frame. Such frames can be genre based (melodrama, films targeted specifically at a female audience, the female buddy movies), auteur based (such as women in the films of Gillian Armstrong), issue based (*The Accused* (Kaplan 1988) for example, is *about* two women's struggle), and so on. This is all well established in various film theory and analysis work. Feminist film theory in the 1970s and 1980s was particularly astute in showing how the absence of women in mainstream cinema prevented an articulation of women's desire. However, what is significant to note is that the development of various versions of 'women's films' does not necessarily mean an end to the invisibility of women in mainstream cinema. The issue is beyond a sort of demarcation of films that are directly marketed to women; in other words a visual culture of women in cinema.

Feminist theory from the 1970s onwards constantly grappled with the difficulty of all this. Basically the various feminist movements (from the Anglo-American groups developed through the ideas of people such as Kate Millet to the French-Continental works of Kristeva, Luce Irigaray, and Hélène Cixous) engaged in strategies to render the invisibility of women (and especially women's desires) impossible. Part of this process was to show the devices of repression that existed in the phallocentric cultural order, including the visual representations of women.

From this theoretical and textual platform gender studies developed, in part from feminist theory, but also through the emergence of masculinity studies and queer theory. A common theme running through these critical approaches was how different sexualities (that is, different from the phallocentric, hetero-normative praxis) were made invisible, and how they struggled for representation outside of their own discourses. It really was often just a case of getting an image of these sexualities constructed and presented. Here we see the significance of Foucault, for through his ideas on the history of sexuality there developed an understanding of power and knowledge as it comes to determine what is to be seen as normal and what is to be excluded, that is, as deviant.

Women, different versions of masculinity, and homosexuality shared the double difficulties; for not only did they have to engage in the whole problematical agenda of sexuality (the history of repression can be traced through the formations of sexuality) but also of a different sort of sexuality. Desire became the formulating principle of subjectivity – one could not exist without the other. And this is the crucial point here. To make a certain version of sexuality (and desire) invisible is also to make a form of subjectivity invisible. There cannot exist a subject of 'woman' or 'gay' unless there also exists a visual culture of that sexuality and desire.

This raises the whole issue of the currency of the image – something we observed earlier in the context of Baudrillard. To create an image of female desire, or active gay and lesbian sexuality, is not only about depicting such acts. It is also about constructing spectators of such images. Herein lies the circle that has proven to be a deeply complex and difficult concern. The image and spectator create each other, and so which must come first? Of course, it is very much a process of gradual developments and moments; the tolerance towards, and profusion of, gay images, for example, in recent years (for example the huge popularity of the television show *Queer as Folk*) comes out of the creation of a type of spectator, which in turn allows for the development of more images. What is essential to such a process is the exchange of images, and so the creation of a visual culture – in this case one of different desires.

The other part of this exchange process is one of pleasure. The spectator and image are involved in a relationship of mutual pleasures. In these terms we cannot take a simple sense of pleasure, but one that is closer to Freud, and even Foucault, and one certainly developed in the theorizing of gender and sexuality. This is seeing pleasure as something that is not necessarily enjoyable. It is something tinged with *jouissance*, evoking potential development and escape, and providing alternatives to the status quo. This is the sense of pleasure as a type of rupture and disquiet, it is the image as it offers the unhinging of the self. This is the pleasure that threatens to disrupt the social order, often challenging the moral and ethical laws. It is a necessary pleasure because it contains within it the seeds of change and potentiality.

Groups that are othered are rendered invisible and so denied the capacity to create images of themselves that can circulate across the cultural order. This ability to generate the visible is part of the processes of pleasure because it is also about the formation and articulation of subjectivity. Of course women, different versions of masculinity, and homosexuality exist, but when they are made invisible the struggle becomes the right to produce images, and therefore become part of the visual culture. Such a struggle accounts for some of the visual flamboyance that takes place when such groups are shown in the hegemonic social order. Gay and lesbian Mardi Gras, steroid bodies and muscle shows, and the acute emotions in melodrama are all part of an assertion of the hyper-image to make these forms of gender and sexuality more visible.

THE INVISIBLE OTHER/THE OTHERING OF INVISIBILITY
Gender and sexuality are good examples of this process of denying the presence of elements within the visual culture (and therefore the wider cultural order) because sexuality itself is something that is constantly problematized within the cultural order. It thus becomes a double agenda when what is at hand is a sexuality that is defined as different. It is the invisibility of such groups that makes them the Other, and so the image becomes a site where all sorts of issues are contested and played out. The legitimacy of existence, the sense of the subject, the capacity to desire and have pleasure, become invested in the visual because of this Othering by invisibility. Similarly, the image becomes a way in which the dominant legitimations, subjectivities, desires and pleasures are sustained. For as long as an image circulates within the culture, and has this powerful currency, whatever is attached to it remains powerful. In this way all images operate within an order of the Same, and all invisibilities operate within a sense of the Other.

We are using 'invisibilities' in quite a specific way here. It is something informed by a great many arguments and ideas that have been discussed in this book, including the rhizome and the simulacra, the assertion of the hyper-image, and so on. 'Invisibilities' does not necessarily mean the literally unseen, but it does acknowledge that spectators do not see everything before their eyes. When most affluent Westerners walk down a busy street in a large city (London, New York, Paris) they see the street beggars enough not to step on them, but the homeless and poor are invisible within the currency of images in their world. Delacroix's paintings of North Africa[d] showed a world of invisibilities to the West; and the way he created the images – so exotic, sexual and violent – confirmed a political visibility of colonialism.[10] The theory of post-colonialism has been organized around examining these sorts of representations, acknowledging how they created an invisible reality and a visible unreality.

We are not so far from Baudrillard's simulacra here. If the Gulf War did not take place, then we can also say that certain genders and sexual practices do not exist, Morocco is an imaginary place, and there is no poverty and homelessness in a large city. These are the invisible Others that are excluded from the hegemonic cultural order by their lack of images. How to make one's self visible, how to have images that can operate within the economy of the cultural order, is the crucial strategy for any group, any subjectivity, any form of desire.

STRATEGIES FOR THE VISIBLE

One of the counters to this force of being made the Other is in fact not to resist it directly. One of the most effective weapons of any resistance group has been its very invisibility. The strategy of the French feminists has been to work within the dominant culture of philosophy and psychoanalysis (take on Hegel and Freud as it were) to produce a different sort of visibility. There are of course dangers with such a positioning – the struggle for visibility by cultural groups, such as African-Americans, sometimes leads to a warping of the image. The television shows of the 1980s and 1990s (such as *The Cosby Show*) produced a type of visibility, but it was a distinctly framed white version. Another example, also from television, is the two gay men in *Will and Grace*. Jack and Will are versions of gayness that perform no more than what the dominant heterosexual culture expects of such men – one flamboyant and camp, the other neat and fastidious. The show does create an image of gayness within the mainstream culture, but it is one that also allows an invisibility to continue to operate. It is, of course, a sitcom, so the audience does not expect a great deal of social commentary, overt sexuality or profound questioning of ethical issues. Such is the visibility of this gayness that it succeeds in maintaining part of the invisibility of that sexuality.

The volatility of the image is part of its strength as a political tool. However, the real strategy for engaging with the processes of the invisible Other and the visible Same rests in the formation of the spectator. When we sit and watch *Will and Grace* we have already framed it within a certain set of discourses (late capitalist US, mainstream television, genre of sitcom, even the time it is shown on television) and so our expectations have been formulated. The fact that it is so popular and successful does give force to the visuality of homosexuality within all those preconditions and discourses. So the spectator and image have settled into a comfortable relationship, both knowing (if one can use such a difficult term) what is expected of them. This is the pleasure of the work, as Barthes puts it.

However, the spectator must also be able to make visible all those elements within the image that extend beyond this simple and comforting pleasure. They must be able to see the invisibilities, acknowledge that they are not there, and admit that it is because of their absence that what is being seen can exist. The gay sexual (and even romantic) acts of both Jack and Will in *Will and Grace* are mostly absent. The spectator knows that they are gay because we are told it, rather than actually shown it (how many times do we actually see physical contact between two men, let alone kissing and other acts of passion?); this is the same in *The Cosby Show* where the spectator sees African-American actors, but within what has usually been seen as a white, middle-class environment. And, as a final example, when Delacroix shows the women of North Africa as exotic and sexual the spectator needs to balance the colonialist sentiments alongside the pleasurable excesses of allowing sexuality to be represented at all.

Visual cultures, then, are never simply about the image. An essential part of the whole process of images being produced, circulating, having currency and force, rests very much in the formation of the spectator. Each of the theorists, and all of the ideas, we have considered in this book have, in one way or another, come back to this fundamental idea. Just as we can say that a visual culture produces a spectator, in equal force the spectator produces visual cultures. Enmeshed in all this are the recurring themes of critical theory – the subject, desire, power, culture and knowledge.

Notes

1 Another way of looking at this would be through the changing attitude towards portraits in painting. Picasso's portraits are extraordinary because they deconstruct not just the style of portrait painting, but also the idea that we are uniform and united subjects. His portraits of Dora Maar, for example, show a multi-faced subject. A painter such as Dürer is noted for his detailed self-portraits, starting at the age of just fourteen and constantly produced into his old age. The self-portraits of Dürer are noteworthy in part because of their detail as a record.

2 Deleuze and Guattari acknowledge this literary bias and talk about the root-book (*livre-racine*) and the literary machine (see, for example, *On the Line*); and yet there are many visual examples and references to their works. So our 'translation' of rhizomes here is not as excessive as may at first seem to be the case; indeed the very metaphor of the rhizome is a strongly visual one.

3 Foucault, in his foreward to *Anti-Oedipus*, described the work as 'an Introduction to the Non-Fascist Life' (Deleuze and Guattari 1984: xiii), arguing 'How does one keep from being a fascist, even (especially) when one believes oneself to be revolutionary militant? … Deleuze and Guattari, for their part, pursue the slightest traces of fascism in the body' (Deleuze and Guattari 1984: xiii).

4 These are cities that clearly have different histories and cultural spaces, and yet also share a great many features (such as late capitalism, Western, two – Boston and Sydney – have similar population sizes, and so on). However, they work as examples of a particular type of city. This rhizome analysis could be done with non-Western cities, smaller spaces, but the points remain essentially the same.

5 The idea of territory here clearly has links to the way we might normally think about meaning and function. Deleuze and Guattari are giving a language-based idea much more of a spatial inflection here.

6 Perhaps one of the most striking aspects of this description of the rhizome is that it echoes the style of writing of Deleuze and Guattari themselves. When they urge 'to write, form rhizomes, expand your own territory by deterritorialization, extend the line of flight to the point where it covers the whole plane of consistency in an abstract machine' (Deleuze and Guattari 1983: 23) we realize that what we are reading is what they are specifying. In this way they have turned their own writings into the very project they are articulating. It is why so much of the style of their works is so rupturing of the disciplines from which it originates – philosophy, social sciences and psychoanalysis. In turn they are suggesting a variation on Surrealism's techniques to produce ideas through contrast and shock. As at one point they admit, 'We are writing this book as a rhizome' (Deleuze and Guattari 1983: 5).

7 Later Deleuze and Claire Parnet compare this sort of cartography to work done on autism in children. They extend the idea of the autistic movements of the body to be a type of map of all movements of all bodies. See 'Politics' by Deleuze and Parnet, esp. pp. 76–7.

8 This is the famous 'metaphor' of Plato's cave, which argues that we are all spectators looking at shadows on a cave wall. Behind us, and away from our direct gaze, exists the original from which this shadow is cast. The essential aspect of this for Plato – and for the thousands of years that followed – was that there must be an essential form from which such shadows originate. For Baudrillard there is no essential form, just shadows.

9 These are brought together in the collection entitled *The Gulf War Did Not Take Place*.

10 For an excellent analysis of this type of analysis see Edward Said, *Orientalism*.

a   Picasso's 'repainting', *Les Ménines*, of Velázquez's *Las Meninas*
http://www.yatrides.com/anglais/others/Velasquez_Picasso.htm

b   Magritte, *Décalcomanie* (1966)
http://www.civil.ubc.ca/home/steph/magritte.html

c   da Vinci, *Mona Lisa*
http://www.louvre.fr/anglais/collec/peint/inv0779/peint_f.htm

d   Delacroix, example of his work on North African women
http://www.ibiblio.org/wm/paint/auth/delacroix/algerian.jpg

BIBLIOGRAPHY

Bakhtin, Mikhail (1968) *Rabelais and his World*, trans. H. Iswolsky, Cambridge, Mass.: MIT Press.

Barthes, Roland (1964) *Essais critiques*, Paris: Seuil.

—— (1967) *Elements of Semiology*, trans. A. Lavers and C. Smith, London: Jonathan Cape.

—— (1973) *Mythologies*, trans. A. Lavers, London: Jonathan Cape.

—— (1974) *S/Z*, trans. R. Howard, New York: Hill and Wang.

—— (1975) *The Pleasure of the Text*, trans. R. Miller, New York: Hill and Wang.

—— (1977) *Image-Music-Text*, trans. S. Heath, Glasgow: Fontana.

—— (1979) *The Eiffel Tower and Other Mythologies*, trans. R. Howard, New York: Hill and Wang.

—— (1984) *Camera Lucida*, trans. R. Howard, London: Flamingo.

—— (1985) *The Grain of the Voice: Interviews 1962–1980*, trans. L. Cloverdale, New York: Hill and Wang.

—— (1990) *The Fashion System*, trans. M. Ward and R. Word, California: University of California Press.

—— (1993) *A Roland Barthes Reader*, ed. S. Sontag, London: Vintage.

Baudrillard, Jean (1982) *In the Shadow of the Silent Majorities*, New York: Semiotext(e).

—— (1983) *Simulations*, trans. P. Beitchman, New York: Semiotext(e).

—— (1988) *The Ecstasy of Communication*, trans. B. and C. Schutze, New York: Semiotext(e).

—— (1990) *Seduction*, trans. B. Singer, London: Macmillan Press.

—— (1995) *The Gulf War Did Not Take Place*, trans. P. Patton, Sydney: Power Publications.

Bazin, Germain (1964) *Baroque and Rococo*, trans. J. Griffin, Norwich: Thames and Hudson.

Benjamin, Walter (1996) *Illuminations: Essays and Reflections*, London: Random House.

Bryson, Norman (1985) *Vision and Painting: The Logic of the Gaze*, Houndmills, Basingstoke, Hampshire: Macmillan Press.

—— (2001) 'Semiology and Visual Interpretation', in Julia Thomas (ed.), *Reading Images*, Houndmills, Basingstoke, Hampshire: Palgrave.

Deleuze, Giles and Félix Guattari (1983) *On the Line*, trans. J. Johnston, New York: Semiotext(e).

—— (1984) *Anti-Oedipus: Capitalism and Schizophrenia*, trans. R. Hurley, M. Seem and H.R. Lane, London: Athlone Press.

Derrida, Jacques (1973) *Speech and Phenomena and Other Essays on Husserl's Theory of Signs*, trans. D.B. Allinson, Evanston: North-Western University Press.

—— (1976) *Of Grammatology*, trans. G.C. Spivak, Baltimore: Johns Hopkins University Press.

—— (1978) *Writing and Difference*, trans. A. Bass, London: Routledge and Kegan Paul.

—— (1979) *Spurs: Nietzsche's Styles*, trans. B. Harlow, Chicago: University of Chicago Press.

—— (1981) *Dissemination*, trans. B. Johnson, London: Athlone Press.

—— (1986) *Margins of Philosophy*, trans. A. Bass, Sussex: Harvester Press.

—— (1987a) *The Post Card: From Socrates to Freud and Beyond*, trans. A. Bass, Chicago: University of Chicago Press.

—— (1987b) *The Truth in Painting*, trans. G. Bennington and I. McLeod, Chicago: University of Chicago Press.

—— (1990) *Memoirs of the Blind*, trans. P.A. Brault and M. Naas, Chicago: University of Chicago Press.

—— (1993) 'Interview' in *Deconstruction and the Visual Arts/Architecture*, ed. P. Brunette and D. Wills, New York: Cambridge.

—— (1994a) 'Sending: On Representation', trans. P. and M.A. Caws, in Patrick Fuery (ed.), *Representation, Discourse and Desire: Contemporary Australian Culture and Critical Theory*, Melbourne: Longman Chesire, pp. 9–34.

—— (1994b) *Spectres of Marx*, trans. P. Kamuf, London: Routledge.

—— (1996) *The Gift of Death*, trans. D. Wills, Chicago: University of Chicago Press.

—— (1997) *Politics of Friendship*, trans. G. Collins, London: Verso.

—— (1998) *Resistances*, trans. P. Kamuf, P.A. Brault and M. Naas, California: Stanford University Press.

—— and Marie-Françoise Plissart (1989) 'Droit de regards', trans. D. Wills, *Art and Text* 32, pp. 19–97.

Eco, Umberto (1976) *A Theory of Semiotics*, Bloomington: Indiana University Press.

—— (1979) *The Role of the Reader*, Bloomington: Indiana University Press.

—— (1984) *Semiotics and the Philosophy of Language*, Bloomington: Indiana University Press.

Foucault, Michel (1970) *The Order of Things*, London: Tavistock.

—— (1975) *The Birth of the Clinic: An Archaeology of Medical Perception*, trans. A.M. Sheridan Smith, New York: Vintage Books.

—— (1979) *The History of Sexuality, Vol. 1*, trans. R. Hurley, New York: Vintage Books.

—— (1983a) 'The Subject in Power', in *Michel Foucault: Beyond Structuralism and Hermeneutics*, Chicago: University of Chicago Press.

—— (1983b) *This is not a Pipe*, trans. J. Harleness, Berkeley: University of California Press.

—— (1986a) *The Archaeology of Knowledge*, trans. A.M. Sheridan Smith, London: Tavistock.

—— (1986b) *The Foucault Reader*, ed. P. Rabinow, Harmondsworth, Middlesex: Penguin.

—— (1987) *Discipline and Punish: The Birth of the Prison*, trans. A.M. Sheridan, London: Allen Lane.

—— (2000) *Ethics, Subjectivity and Truth, Vol. 1*, trans. R. Hurley *et al.*, Harmondsworth, Middlesex: Penguin.

—— (2000) *Aesthetics, Method and Epistemology, Vol. 2*, trans. R. Hurley *et al.*, Harmondsworth, Middlesex: Penguin.

—— (2002) *Power, Vol. 3*, trans. R. Hurley *et al.*, Harmondsworth, Middlesex: Penguin.

Freud, Sigmund (1977) *On Sexuality*, trans. J. Strachey, Harmondsworth, Middlesex: Penguin.

—— (1984) *On Psychopathology*, trans. J. Strachey, Harmondsworth, Middlesex: Penguin.

—— (1985) *Case Studies 1: 'Dora' and 'Little Hans'*, trans. J. Strachey, Harmondsworth, Middlesex: Penguin.

—— (1986) *The Interpretation of Dreams*, trans. J. Strachey, Harmondsworth, Middlesex: Penguin.

—— (1987) *On Metapsychology: The Theory of the Unconscious*, trans. J. Strachey, Harmondsworth, Middlesex: Penguin.

—— (1988) *The Psychopathology of Everyday Life*, trans. J. Strachey, Harmondsworth, Middlesex: Penguin.

—— (1990a) *Art and Literature*, trans. J. Strachey, Harmondsworth, Middlesex: Penguin.

—— (1990b) *Totem and Taboo*, trans. J. Strachey, New York: W.W. Norton and Company.

—— (1991) *Civilization, Society and Religion*, trans. J. Strachey, Harmondsworth, Middlesex: Penguin.

Fuery, Patrick (1995) *The Theory of Absence*, Westport: Greenwood Press.

—— (2000) *New Developments in Film Theory*, London: Macmillan Press.

Guattari, Felix (1984) *Molecular Revolution: Psychiatry and Politics*, trans. R. Sheed, Harmondsworth, Middlesex: Penguin.

—— (1995) *Chaosmosis: An Ethico-Aesthetic Paradigm*, trans. P. Bains and J. Pefanis, Sydney: Power Publications.

Heidegger, Martin (1962) *Being and Time*, trans. J. Macquarrie and E. Robinson, London: SCM Press.

Kristeva, Julia (1982) *Powers of Horror: An Essay on Abjection*, trans. L.S. Roudiez, New York: Columbia University Press.

—— (1984a) *Desire in Language: A Semiotic Approach to Literature and Art*, trans. T. Gora, A. Jardine and L. Roudiez, Oxford: Basil Blackwell.

—— (1984b) *Revolution in Poetic Language*, trans. M. Walter, New York: Columbia University Press.

—— (1986a) 'Ellipsis on Dread and the Specular Seduction', in P. Rosen (ed.), *Narrative, Apparatus Ideology: A Film Theory Reader*, New York: Columbia University Press.

—— (1986b) 'The System and the Speaking Subject' in Toril Moi (ed.), *The Kristeva Reader*, New York: Columbia University Press.

Lacan, Jacques (1975a) 'Seminar on *The Purloined Letter*', in *Yale French Studies* 52, pp. 38–72.

—— (1975b) *Livre XX: Encore 1972–1973*, Paris: Seuil.

—— (1985) *Écrits: A Selection*, trans. A. Sheridan, London: Tavistock.

—— (1986) *The Four Fundamental Concepts of Psychoanalysis*, trans. A. Sheridan, Harmondsworth, Middlesex: Penguin.

—— (1988a) *Freud's Papers on Technique 1953–1954*, trans. J. Forrester, ed. J.-A. Miller, Cambridge: Cambridge University Press.

—— (1988b) *The Ego in Freud's Theory and in the Technique of Psychoanalysis 1954–1955*, trans. S. Tomaselli, ed. J.-A. Miller, Cambridge: Cambridge University Press.

—— (1992) *The Ethics of Psychoanalysis 1959–1960*, trans. D. Porter, ed. J.-A. Miller, London: Routledge.

—— (1993) *The Psychoses 1955–1960*, trans. R. Grigg, ed. J.-A. Miller, London: Routledge.

—— (1998) *On Feminine Sexuality: The Limits of Love and Knowledge 1972–1973*, trans. Bruce Fink, ed. J.-A. Miller, New York: W.W. Norton and Company.

Lechte, John (1990) *Julia Kristeva*, London: Routledge.

Lyotard, Jean-François (1985) *The Postmodern Condition: A Report on Knowledge*, trans. G. Bennington and B. Massumi, Manchester: Manchester University Press.

—— (1993) *Libidinal Economy*, trans. I. Hamilton Grant, Bloomington: Indiana University Press.

Moi, Toril (1985) *Sexual/Textual Politics: Feminist Literary Theory*, London and New York: Methuen.

Poe, Edgar Allen (1966) *The Purloined Letter*, New York: Franklin Watts Inc.

Said, Edward (1978) *Orientalism*, New York: Random House.

INDEX

Thurman, Una 70, 85
Titian 74, 85
trace, the 65–6, 117–18
transgression 53–4, 65–6
Treachery of Images, The (Magritte) 90, 96, 108
t-shirts, Westwood 102, 108
Tura, Cosimo 4, 20
Turn of the Screw, The (James) 79
TV Dante, A (Greenaway) 95
Twin Peaks (Lynch) 3, 19
Twin Towers disaster 68–9, 110–11
Two Mysteries, The (Magritte) 90, 108

unclean, the 58–9
unnameable, the 46–8

Valentino, Rudolph 38
Van Eyck, Jan 83, 85
Van Gogh, Vincent 72, 85
Velázquez, Diego
    Las Meninas 17, 21, 113
    Rokeby Venus 9, 21, 70, 84
Venus 70–1, 84
virology 65–8
voice, the 100

Warhol, Andy 9, 20, 60, 95
Westwood, Vivienne 102, 108
Wild at Heart (Lynch) 3
Will and Grace 126
Willis, Bruce 39
Withnail and I (Robinson) 14